IPHONE 14

SENIORS GUIDE

Learn How to Use Your New iPhone
in Just 30 Minutes a Day with This Complete
and Easy Manual for Seniors, Tech-savvy or Not.
With Settings to Make the iPhone Easier to Use.

HENRY SANDERS

TABLE OF CONTENTS

INTRODUCTION

UNBOXING TOGETHER: WHAT IS INSIDE YOUR NEW IPHONE'S BOX + EXTRA TOOLS THAT CAN BE BOUGHT.

The Apple iPhone 14, a USB Type C to Lightning cable that supports rapid charging and is compatible with USB-C power adapters and computer connections, and the accompanying documentation are all included in the package that the iPhone 14 comes in. As Apple works toward its goal of becoming carbon neutral by the year 2030, the company has decided to stop include the power adapter and the EarPods with the iPhone 14 Pro and Pro Max.

For the extra tools that you want to buy, these could be iPhone accessories such as cases and etc.

MODELS

Apple's new "cheap" flagship iPhones, the iPhone 14 and iPhone 14 Plus, are being marketed alongside the company's more expensive iPhone 14 Pro and Pro Max models. The iPhone 14 and Plus are referred to as Apple's "affordable" flagship iPhones. The "small" iPhone was discontinued by Apple in 2022, and the new iPhone 14 versions are available in 6.1-inch and 6.7-inch screen sizes. The new iPhone 14, which has a screen size of 6.7 inches, is being marketed as the "iPhone 14 Plus," a name that references previous iterations of the iPhone, including the iPhone 8 and iPhone 8 Plus. The design of Apple's iPhone 14 models is the same as the design of Apple's iPhone 13 models. Both models include flat corners, a casing made of aerospace-grade aluminum, and a glass back that allows for wireless charging.

The new iPhone 14 versions sold in the United States do not include a slot for SIM cards. The most recent models have a variety of enhancements, such as the new Dynamic Island, an A16 Bionic chip, updated cameras, and other features. Both the iPhone 14 and the iPhone 14 Plus are, in all material respects, the same phone; the only difference is the size of the display. The iPhone 14 Pro and the iPhone 14 Pro Max are identical in terms of the components that go into their production; the only distinguishing feature between the two is that one of them is noticeably larger than the other.

You won't notice a significant difference in the device's general design or functionality when you upgrade from an iPhone 14 to another model of the iPhone 14. These two upgrades take place simultaneously. The upgrade from an iPhone 14 to iPhone 14 Pro is a major one in terms of the capabilities available and the cost. Despite the fact that both devices have dimensions that are nearly the same, the overall experience will be significantly different if the user upgrades from an iPhone 14 Plus to an iPhone 14 Pro Max. This is the case even though the two devices have nearly the same dimensions.

Differences between the standard iPhone 14 and iPhone 14 Plus, as well as the iPhone 14 Pro and iPhone 14 Pro Max are as follows:

• Differences in the dimensions of the display and the overall chassis size: Plus and Pro Max are both larger

• There is a variation in the battery size: the iPhone Plus and Pro Max models have a larger battery, which allows them to have a longer run time but also requires more time to charge.

A brand new always-on display is utilized by both the iPhone 14 Pro and the iPhone 14 Pro Max. Because of this, your iPhone is able to show particular widgets, such as the current time or the weather, even while the screen of the phone is off. It preserves the life of your battery while also keeping you up to date.

DESIGN

It has a textured matte glass back, a stainless steel design, and a Ceramic Shield front that is applied to the front glass to improve its longevity. It features a new dual-camera system, Crash Detection, a smartphone industry-first safety service with Emergency SOS via satellite, and the best battery life on iPhone. It comes in a larger 6.7-inch version that joins the existing 6.1-inch design.

The new Main and front TrueDepth cameras, the UltraWide camera for capturing one-of-a-kind viewpoints, and the Photonic Engine, an upgraded picture pipeline, are all included in the powerful camera system that the iPhone 14 and iPhone 14 Plus use to create breathtaking images and videos. Both versions come equipped with Apple's A15 Bionic CPU, which features a 5-core graphics processing unit (GPU).

This chip not only provides exceptional performance and efficiency even while working with heavy tasks, but it also incorporates privacy and security features into its architecture. The Crash Detection and Emergency SOS via Satellite features on the iPhone 14 and iPhone 14 Plus are a first for the mobile industry.

These features are introduced with the iPhone 14 and iPhone 14 Plus. This year's array of iPhones is our most technologically sophisticated yet, largely thanks to their incredible battery life, features that top the industry in terms of durability, and lightning-fast 5G connectivity.

COLOR

- The available colors are blue, purple, midnight, starlight, and product (red).

SHELL RESISTANCE and WATER RESISTANCE

- The iPhone 14 and 14 Plus both have a classification of IP68, which indicates that they are resistant to the incursion of water and dust. Cell phones can endure being submerged in water for up to half an hour at a depth of up to six meters (19.7 feet). The number "6" in "IP68" refers to the device's resistance to dust (which indicates that it can withstand dirt, dust, and other particulates), while the number "8" refers to the device's resistance to water. The IP6x designation represents the highest level of protection against dust that may be achieved. With a classification of IP68, the iPhone 14 is protected against water damage caused by splashes, rain, and unintentional immersion in water; nonetheless, water immersion should be avoided when possible. According to Apple, resistance to water and dust is not permanent; it may diminish over time due to natural wear and use. Because Apple's basic warranty does not cover damage caused by liquids, it is essential to exercise extreme caution when it comes to being exposed to fluids.

STORAGE

The kinds of files and applications that we store on our iPhones continue to expand in size as the devices become more sophisticated. This indicates that you will need a sufficient amount of storage space on the device's internal memory in order to save all of the photos, videos, and applications that you want to save.

At the time of purchase for your iPhone 14, you will be prompted to select the amount of internal storage space that you require. The greater the quantity that you order, the higher the price will be.

There are 128GB, 256GB, and 512GB storage capacities available for each of the four different iPhone 14 models. The majority of users will not need more space than what is provided by these options, particularly those with 256GB or more.

On the contrary, the iPhone 14 Pro and Pro Max models both come with an even more impressive 1TB storage capacity as an option. This offers approximately the same amount of storage as the 512GB model, which is just about twice as much.

BATTERY

There is a difference in the amount of battery life provided by each model of the iPhone 14.

According to Apple, the iPhone 14 has the shortest battery life, followed by the iPhone 14 Pro, then iPhone 14 Plus, and the iPhone 14 Pro Max. To put it another way, the larger batteries found in the two largest iPhone models are the most powerful.

The iPhone 14 has a battery life of 20 hours, the iPhone 14 Pro has a battery life of 23 hours, the iPhone 14 Plus has a battery life of 26 hours, and the iPhone 14 Pro Max has a battery life of 29 hours if video is left playing continuously. This indicates that the iPhone should be able to withstand normal usage conditions for an even greater amount of time.

Each and every model of the iPhone 14 supports charging via wireless charging, charging via MagSafe magnetic charging, and fast charging with an adapter that can provide 20W.

WHAT IS NEW?

- Although the iPhone 14 and iPhone 14 Plus from Apple may appear to be visually identical to the iPhone 13 series from the previous year, numerous improvements have been made to the internal components of both models. The iPhone 14 line includes new sensors for auto-crash detection. Another is the method for processing photographs known as the Photonic Engine and the elimination of a physical SIM card slot for phones sold in the United States and the improvements to the cameras located on the back and the front of the device. The most noticeable change, however, pertains to the phone line's sizes: the Mini version is no longer available as part of the iPhone 14 range; instead, a standard phone with a display of 6.1 inches is being released alongside a Plus model that has an array of 6.7 inches.

The majority of the new features that were introduced with the iPhone 14, such as emergency satellite connections, automobile crash detection, and a "Action" filming mode that keeps the camera stable, are going to be available on all four models. However, there are a few exclusive features that are only available to those who have purchased the Pro or Pro Max version.

First, the Pro and the Pro Max each incorporate a LiDAR scanner within their respective cameras. You can create incredibly precise representations of anything in your environment with LiDAR by just pointing your camera in its direction. This technology is similar to radar in several ways. This is fantastic for augmented reality apps, such as ones that enable you to position virtual things in the room that actually exists in your world.

To continue with the camera, both the Pro and the Pro Max can record videos in Apple's own ProRes format.

All of this is achieved by a brand new A16 Bionic chip that is housed inside both the Pro and the Pro Max. This chip is responsible for the operation of almost every component of the iPhone, including the display of images and the operation of applications.

The A16 Bionic represents the most powerful chip that has ever been installed in an iPhone. In contrast, the iPhone 14 and iPhone 14 Plus are equipped with the more mature A15 Bionic chip, which is still extremely competent but operates at a somewhat slower speed.

Finally, the Pro and the Pro Max each have a unique feature that is located at the very top of their respective screens. This feature is called "Dynamic Island," and it was previously described.

The front-facing camera and the facial recognition scanner are housed within the Dynamic Island, which is a little pill-shaped cutout located at the very top of the screen. It is intended to serve as a replacement for the infamous notch that is located at the top of the screen of the normal iPhone 14. However, in contrast to the notch, it is surrounded by functional pixels rather than empty black space.

And it's not only for holding the cameras, either. The Dynamic Island expands and contracts to display a wide variety of data, and its appearance is determined by the apps that you are now using. Because of this, it is also perfect for multitasking, since it may display information from one program while you are using another app at the same time.

The camera has been the feature that has differentiated the majority of iPhone models from one another for many years. You can tell by counting them that the iPhone 14 and 14 Plus only have one camera on the rear, whereas the iPhone Pro and Pro Max each have three.

However, these distinctions go far beyond than that. The main and ultra-wide cameras on the iPhone 14 and 14 Plus both have a resolution of 12 megapixels, while the iPhone 14 Pro and Pro Max have a resolution of 48 megapixels. An additional 12MP telephoto lens is included with both the Pro and Pro Max models. This lens provides up to a 3x optical zoom in and a 2x zoom out.

To put it another way, the Pro and Pro Max cameras are capable of zooming in and out significantly further without degrading the image quality or blurring the details. Both long-distance and close-up photography are simplified as a result. In light of the fact that the Pro and Pro Max cameras have undergone a number of additional internal modifications, including the installation of a brand new A16 processor, these cameras need to be the first choice of photographers.

The front-facing camera on each of the four variants of the iPhone 14 has been upgraded and now features autofocus. This enables the device to capture sharp images of multiple subjects at varying distances simultaneously.

Front-facing camera features

- The front-facing camera on Apple's iPhone 14 models has been upgraded to 12 megapixels. It now has an aperture of 1.9, which is supposed to let in more light than previous models, making it possible to take better selfies and participate in higher-quality FaceTime video chats. It also includes autofocus for the first time, increasing image quality even further, and it takes selfies that are twice as good even in low light.

- The front-facing camera supports many of the same features as the rear cameras, including Night mode for taking selfies, Smart HDR 4, Dolby Vision HDR recording, Deep Fusion, and the new Photonic Engine, in addition to

ProRes and the Cinematic mode for capturing videos with depth-of-field changes that are reminiscent of movies.

Dual Lens Rear Camera

- Apple has upgraded the primary camera to have an aperture of f/1.5, which is an improvement over the aperture of f/1.6 that was utilized in the camera of the iPhone 13. The new lens, which also features a bigger sensor, has a wider aperture, which allows more light to enter the camera and results in an improvement even in low-light settings. Apple claims that the new Main camera can capture 49 percent more light than the camera found in the iPhone 13.

- The Ultra-Wide camera has not been updated, and this model does not come with a telephoto lens like the 14 Pro and 14 Pro Max. The iPhone 14 and 14 Plus only have a maximum optical zoom of 2 times. However, digital zoom can go up to 5 times.

THE BASICS TO KNOW ABOUT APPLE WORLD.

The sustainable environment Apple is dedicated to preserving is firmly embedded in the company's operational procedures. The environmental impact of Apple's operations is carefully considered at every stage, beginning with the earliest stages of product creation and continuing through manufacturing, use, and recycling.

Apple is actively working to enhance its product design, manufacturing processes, energy use, and recycling initiatives through the use of proactive methods. in order to support a healthy environment for everyone. These improvements are made possible by the utilization of renewable energy sources. These steps include: selecting environmentally acceptable materials and substances, reducing waste from the manufacturing process, providing software tools that enable users to control the energy-saving features of their systems, and providing product recycling programs for customers worldwide.

The iPhone and the Environment are designed with the following features to limit the amount of impact they have on the environment:

Made with better materials

- 100% wire made entirely of recycled gold in each and every camera, as well as plating used on a variety of printed circuit boards
- 100 percent recycled tungsten is being used in the Taptic Engine, which accounts for one hundred percent of the tungsten in the iPhone 14 Plus and ninety-nine percent of the tungsten in the iPhone 14.
- 100% recycled rare earth elements in each and every magnet, which accounts for 100% of the rare earth elements found in the iPhone 14 and 99% of the rare earth elements found in the iPhone 14 Plus.
- Multiple printed circuit boards use solder that is composed entirely of recycled tin
- Recycled plastic content of at least 35% across all product components

Energy efficient

- Exceeds the requirements set forth by the United States Department of Energy for battery charger systems

Smarter chemistry

- Glass that is free of arsenic
- Free of Mercury, Beryllium, Brominated Flame Retardants, and PVC

Green manufacturing

- Apple's Zero Waste Program assists third-party vendors in reducing the amount of waste that is disposed of in landfills.
- Every single final assembly supplier facility that Apple uses is currently in the process of switching to 100% renewable energy.

Responsible packaging

- One hundred percent of virgin wood fiber originates from environmentally conscious forest management.
- At least 90 percent of the packaging is made from fiber

Recycling

- Apple adopts a comprehensive approach to the management of materials and the reduction of waste.

CHAPTER 1

THE BASICS

TURN ON AND OFF

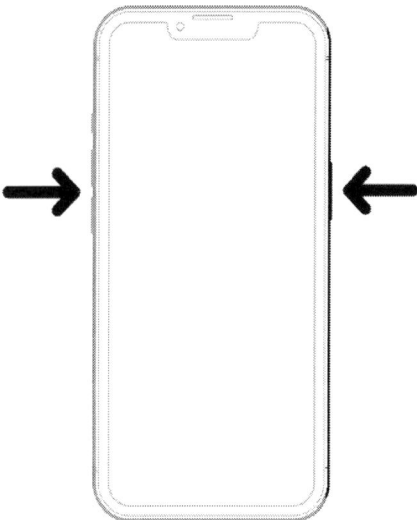

To activate your iPhone, press the button on the side. To power off your iPhone, you may either press the side button (which, on some models, also doubles as one of the volume buttons) or go into Settings.

If your iPhone isn't functioning as planned, you can restart it by powering it down and then back up again. If turning it off and then back on doesn't solve the problem, you might try restarting it manually.

Turn on iPhone

- To bring up the Apple logo, you'll need to press and keep holding the button on the side.

Turn off iPhone

- To turn off Face ID on an iPhone, press and hold the side button as well as either volume button at the same time until the display of the slider, and then move the power Off slider.

- iPhones with a Home button: Move the slider after pressing and holding the side button for a few seconds.

- All models: To shut down your device, navigate to Settings > General > Shut Down, then move the slider.

SET UP YOUR IPHONE

To ensure that the setting up process goes as well as possible, ensure that you have the following items available:

- Either a connection to the internet provided by a Wi-Fi network (for which you will likely require the name and password of the network) or mobile data service provided by a carrier (not required for iPhone 14 models)

- Your old iPhone or a backup of your current device, depending on whether or not you plan to migrate your data to your new iPhone.

- Your Apple ID and password; if you do not already have an Apple ID, you will be prompted to establish one throughout the setup process if you do not already have one.

- Your credit or debit card account information if you want to add a card to Apple Pay during setup.

- The process of transferring your data to your new device can be done while the device is being set up.

A helpful tip is that if you don't have enough storage space to back up your device, iCloud will provide you with as much as you need to perform a temporary backup at no additional cost for up to three weeks after you acquire your iPhone.

This offer is valid from the date you purchase your iPhone.

➢ Go to the Settings menu on your older device, select General, and tap the option to Transfer or Reset [device].

➢ Tap the Get Started button, and then follow the instructions on the screen.

Start setting up your iPhone

1. While pressing your finger against the side button, wait for the Apple logo to show. If you can't get your iPhone to switch on, the battery might need to be charged.

2. Carry out any one of the following actions:

• Select Set Up Manually from the drop-down menu, then adhere to the directions on the screen.

• You can utilize Quick Start to instantly configure your new device if you already own an iOS device (iPhone, iPad, or iPod touch) running iOS 11 or a later version of iOS (iOS 13 or later). Put the two devices close to one another, and then follow the directions on the screen to safely replicate a variety of your settings, including iCloud Keychain. After that, you may use the iCloud backup on the cloud to bring the rest of your data and material over to your new smartphone.

- Alternately, if both of your devices are running iOS 12.4, iPad 13, or a later version, you can wirelessly transfer all of your data from your old device to your new one. Until the migration process is over, keep your electronic gadgets close to one another and plug them into power sources.

- A data transfer can also be performed through a wired connection between the two devices.

•You can activate Voice Over, the screen reader, during the initial setup process if you are blind or have low vision by triple-clicking the side button or triple-clicking the Home button (on other iPhone models). You may also activate Zoom by double-touching the screen while using three fingers.

Move from an Android device to iPhone.

In the initial phase of setting up your new iPhone, if you have an Android device, you can transfer your data via an app called Move to iOS.

Note: If you have previously finished setting up your iPhone and now want to utilize Migrate to iOS, you will need to delete your iPhone and begin the setup process again, or you will need to move your data manually.

1. Carry out the following procedures on your iPhone:

- Be sure to follow the assistant's instructions.
- To move data from Android, hit the Move Data from Android option on the Apps & Data screen.

1. On a smartphone using Android, perform the following steps:

- Make sure that Wi-Fi is turned on.
- Launch the app called Move to iOS.
- Make sure you follow the directions that appear on-screen.

WAKING UP YOUR IPHONE

Wake and unlock iPhone 14.

When you are not using the iPhone, the display will switch off to save battery, the device will lock for more protection, and it will go to sleep. When you are ready to use your iPhone once more, you may easily wake it up and unlock it.

One of the following must be done in order to activate the iPhone:

- To start, press the button on the side.
- Raise iPhone.

Note: If you want to disable Raise to Wake, you can do so by navigating to Settings > Display & Brightness.

- Touch the display (on a supported iPhone model).

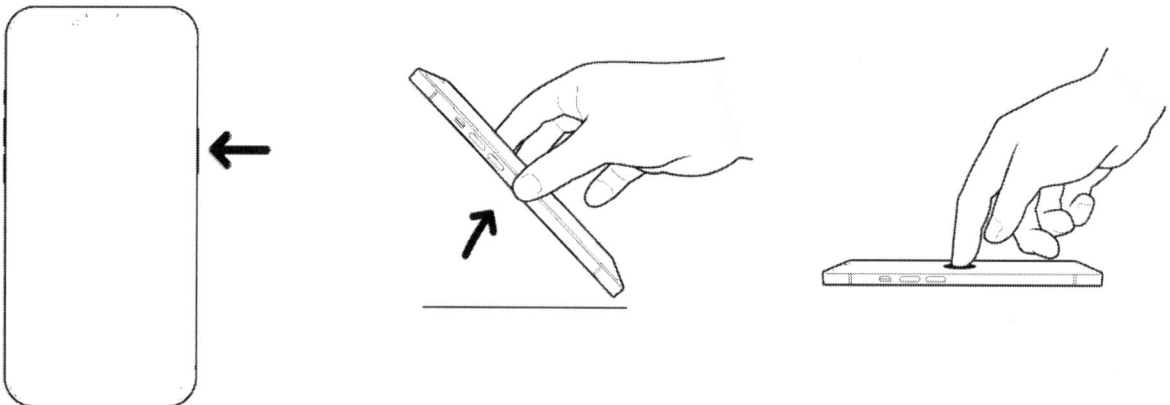

Face ID will allow you to unlock your iPhone.

Move your head slowly to complete the circle.

If you have an iPhone that supports Face ID but you skipped the step during setup that required you to turn it on, check out how to set up the Face ID.

• To wake up your iPhone, either tap the screen or lift it above your head, and then take a quick look at it.

• When an iPhone is unlocked, the lock icon will go through an animation in which it changes from closed to open.

• To access the top of the screen, swipe your finger up from the bottom.

You may re-lock your iPhone by pressing the button on the side. If you don't touch the screen of your iPhone for about a minute, it will lock itself automatically. However, if you go to Settings > Face ID & Passcode and turn on Attention Aware Features, your iPhone won't lock or dim as long as it senses that you are paying attention to it.

Enter your passcode to unlock the iPhone.

See the guide on how to set a passcode on your iPhone if you did not create a passcode when you initially set up your iPhone.

- Swipe up from the bottom of the Lock Screen on an iPhone that has Face ID built in. You'll need to press the Home button on other iPhones.
- Enter your passcode.
- You may re-lock your iPhone by pressing the button on the side. If you don't touch the screen of your iPhone for about a minute, it will lock itself automatically.

Use Raise to Wake

The Lock Screen will automatically become active once you lift your iPhone to your face to look at it. You may quickly check your alerts from there and access the Control Center; swiping left will allow you to take a photo while lifting right will give you access to widgets. In addition, if you have an iPhone newer model, you may tap the screen to check your notifications quickly, take a photo, or use the flashlight.

Swipe up from the bottom of the screen to unlock any iPhone model released after the X. If you're using an iPhone 8 or a model older than that, hit the Home button. Your iPhone will automatically resume its sleep mode if you do nothing to wake it up.

- Go to Settings > Display & Brightness to enable or disable your device's Raise to Wake feature.

The Always-On display is standard on the iPhone 14 Pro and iPhone 14 Pro Max, which is enabled by default. The screen on your iPhone will go darker, but it will continue to show helpful information like the current time, wallpaper, and widgets.

Raise the display of your iPhone to interact with it while the Always-On display is on. You may also interact with the device by tapping the screen or pushing the button on the side of the device. If you have Raised to Wake enabled on your iPhone, simply lifting it to your face and staring at it will wake the device. You may also wake up your iPhone and enable Face ID authentication by swiping your finger upward from the bottom of the display.

CONNECTING YOUR PHONE TO INTERNET 3G/4G/5G AND WI-FI.

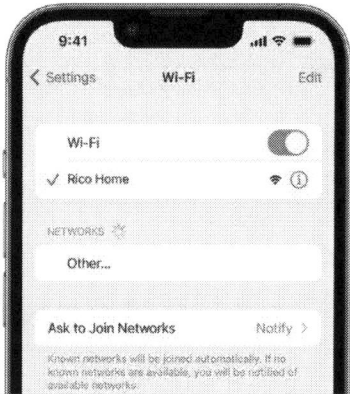

You have the ability to switch cellular data and roaming on or off, select which apps and services utilize cellular data, view your usage of cellular data, and adjust several other parameters related to cellular data.

Note: Please get in touch with your wireless service provider if you need assistance with cellular network services, voicemail, or bills.

In the event when an iPhone is connected to the internet over the cellular data network, the status bar will display an icon that corresponds to the cellular network.

The GSM cellular networks that enable 5G, LTE, 4G, and 3G service also support simultaneous voice and data connections. If your iPhone does not also have a connection to the internet through Wi-Fi, you will not be able to access online services while chatting on the phone if you are using any other type of cellular connection. This is because online services require a connection to the internet. It is possible that you will not be able to receive calls on your iPhone while it is transferring data over the cellular network. For example, if you are downloading a webpage, this could prevent you from receiving calls.

Incoming calls on GSM networks may be sent directly to voicemail while using an EDGE or GPRS connection, depending on the specifics of the connection. Data transfers are put on hold if you pick up an incoming call and answer it.

When you take a call using an EV-DO connection on a CDMA network, the data transfer is interrupted while you take the call. It's possible that incoming calls on 1xRTT connections will be sent straight to voicemail when data is being transferred. Data transfers are put on hold if you pick up an incoming call and answer it.

When you hang up, data transfer picks back up where it left off.
- If you turn off your cellular connection, all of your data services, such as email, online surfing, and push notifications, will only work via Wi-Fi. If Cellular Data is turned on, you may be subject to additional fees from your carrier. For instance, if you use specific features and services that transfer data, like Siri and Messages, you may end up having to pay additional fees for them under your data plan.

Turn on Cellular Data

Simply navigate to Settings > Cellular to enable or disable the Cellular Data service.

Cellular Data Options can be found by navigating to Settings > Cellular > Cellular Data Options. From there, you may choose to do any of the following while Cellular Data is active:

Turning on Low Data Mode will reduce your utilization of cellular data. If you press Data Mode first, then choose Low Data Mode. When your iPhone is not connected to a Wi-Fi network, this mode will suspend any automatic updates and tasks that are running in the background.

Data Roaming enables internet access over a cellular data network when you are in a region that is not covered by the network provided by your carrier. You can choose to turn Data Roaming on or off. You can prevent incurring roaming charges by switching off data roaming while you are away from home.

The following configuration choices may be accessible on your iPhone, depending on its model, its network provider, and its location:

To activate or deactivate voice roaming: (CDMA) Turn off Voice Roaming to avoid incurring additional fees as a result of using the networks of other carriers.

The iPhone will not have cellular service (either data or voice) while the network provided by your carrier is unavailable.

Turn on or turn off 4G/LTE: Using 4G or LTE may load internet data more quickly in some instances, but it may also degrade the performance of the battery. There is a chance that there will be options to switch off 4G/LTE, pick Voice & Data (VoLTE), or select Data Only.

Connect to the 3G/ 4G/ 5G network.

1. Go to settings

2. Select Mobile Data

3. Make your selections for Mobile Data.

4. Select Voice & Data

5. To enable 3G, pick 3G. The same applies to 4G; select 4G from the menu to activate it. The same can be said about the 5G standard.

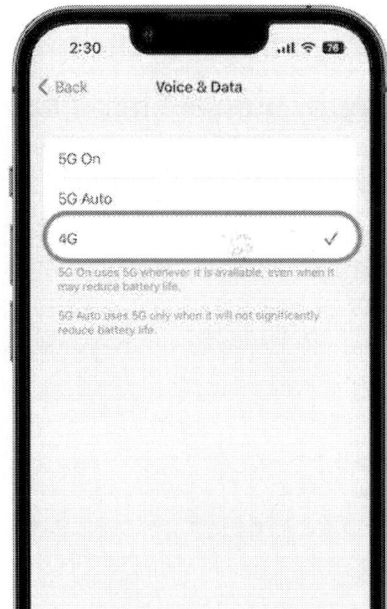

Connect iPhone to a Wi-Fi network

- Navigate to Settings > Wi-Fi from the Home screen of your device.
- Make sure the Wi-Fi is turned on. Your device will perform a search for available Wi-Fi networks on its own automatically.
- Simply select the Wi-Fi hotspot that you wish to join by tapping its name. It is possible that you will need to enter the network's password or agree to the terms and conditions before you can become a member of the network.
- Once you've successfully joined the network, you'll notice a blue checkmark next to the network's name, as well as a connected Wi-Fi symbol in the top right-hand corner of your screen. Get in touch with the person in charge of the network if you are unable to remember the password for the Wi-Fi network.

When you need to connect to the internet, your iPhone will, in order, perform the following steps until a connection is established:

- Makes an attempt to connect to the Wi-Fi network that was used the least recently that is still available.
- Displays a list of available Wi-Fi networks, from which you may select one to join, and then connects to that network.
- Establishes a connection with the cellular data network of your provider

If your iPhone is compatible with 5G, it may switch to using the data from your 5G cellular connection rather than the data from your Wi-Fi connection. If this is the case, you will notice the phrase Using 5G Cellular for Internet below the name of the Wi-Fi network. Tap the Info button next to the network name, and then tap the Use Wi-Fi for Internet option. This will switch you back to using Wi-Fi. Check out the page titled "Use 5G with your iPhone" on the Apple Support website.

Note that in the event that a connection to the internet via Wi-Fi is unavailable, some apps and services may choose to transfer data via your cellular network instead, which may result in additional charges being incurred. Get more information about your cellular data rates by getting in touch with your carrier.

MIGRATING YOUR DATA

Quick Start requires the usage of both devices; you should schedule it when you will only need the assistance of the one you are now working on for at least a few minutes.

1. Start up your new technology and position it next to the one you already use. To get started, follow the on-screen directions. In the event that the prompt to set up your new device on your existing device is no longer visible, you will be required to restart both of your devices.

2. Connect your device to a wireless network, either Wi-Fi or the cellular network that comes with your smartphone.

3. It is possible that you will be requested to activate your cellular service.

4. Activate either Face ID or Touch ID.

5. Decide how you want to go about transferring your data.

    • When you download from iCloud, your apps and data will download in the background so that you can immediately begin using your new device.

    • If you transfer directly from the device you were using previously, you will need to wait until the transfer is finished on both devices before you can use either one of them.

6. Until data migration is finished, keep your electronic gadgets close to one another and plug them into power sources. Several variables can affect how long a transfer takes, including the state of the network and the quantity of data being sent.

SETTING UP SECURITY

Your data and privacy are safeguarded by the iPhone's design. No one else can access the information stored on your iPhone or in iCloud to save you because of the built-in security safeguards. You have the ability to change what information is shared and where you share it, in addition to built-in privacy safeguards that reduce the amount of your data that is accessible to anyone other than you.

If you follow these best practices, you will get the most out of the safety and privacy features built into your iPhone.

Lock down access to your Apple iPhone.

- Create a secure passcode: The essential step you can do to ensure the safety of your iPhone is to enable the use of a passcode whenever it has to be unlocked.

- Use Face ID or Touch ID: Using Face ID (supported models) or Touch ID (supported models) is a secure and convenient way to unlock your iPhone, authorize purchases and payments, and sign in to many third-party apps. Face ID and Touch ID both require the user to have a camera on the front of their device. Face ID requires that your iPhone have a front-facing camera, while Touch ID requires that your iPhone have a home button. Look at the instructions on how to set up Face ID on an iPhone or how to set up Touch ID on an iPhone.

- When Find My iPhone is activated, it assists you in locating your iPhone if it has been misplaced or stolen and prohibits anybody else from starting or using it if it has gone missing.

- You have complete command over which functionalities are accessible on your iPhone, even if locked. When your device is locked, you can allow or disable access to certain functionalities that are often utilized, such as the Control Center and USB connections.

Maintain the safety of your Apple ID.

- Your Apple ID grants you access to your data stored in iCloud and the account information you need to use Apple services such as the App Store and Apple Music.

Make it simpler and more secure to sign in to accounts.
Signing in to partner websites and apps can be done in several ways, each of which is designed to be more convenient and secure.

- Log in with passkeys. Instead of using a password to access your website and app accounts, you can use passkeys, which let you sign in using Face ID or Touch ID. A Because a passkey doesn't leave the devices where you've signed in with your Apple ID and because it is unique to the website or app that you make it for, it is protected from leaks and attempts to phish it. This is because the passkey doesn't leave the devices where you've signed in with your Apple ID. Passkeys are also specific to the website or app that you make them for. Passkeys are also particular to the website or app you generate. In addition, in contrast to a password, you do not need to render it, guard it, or remember it.

- Go to Settings > iCloud > Sign in with Apple to sign in to accounts; you can use your Apple ID instead of coming up with user names and passwords and having to remember them. Signing in with your Apple account not only gives the added layer of protection that comes with two-factor authentication but also restricts the information that can be shared about you.

- o When you sign up for a service, if the option to use passkey support or Sign in with Apple isn't available, you can use the autofill feature on your iPhone to have it generate a secure password for you that you don't have to remember. This feature is only accessible on iOS devices.

Various other methods available to you can make signing into all of your websites and apps simpler and safer.

- Change compromised passwords: If you make any passwords that are vulnerable to being cracked, your iPhone will notify you automatically so that you can change them.

- Securely share passkeys and passwords: You can safely exchange a passkey or password with another user who has an iPhone, iPad, or Mac by using Apple's AirDrop service.

- For two-factor authentication, use the built-in authenticator. For websites and apps that enable two-factor authentication, fill in the verification codes that are automatically created; do not rely on SMS messages or different apps.

- Quickly enter passcodes for SMS messages: On an iPhone, you can automatically fill in one-time passcodes that are supplied to you from websites or apps.

- Ensure that the passkeys and passwords on all your devices are kept up to date: Your credentials will continuously be updated across all your devices thanks to iCloud Keychain's automated updates.

SETTING UP APPLE PAY + WALLET

Set up Apple Pay in Wallet on iPhone

Apple Pay can be more straightforward and secure than a physical credit card. You can use Apple Pay to make secure payments in stores, for public transit, in apps, and on websites that support Apple Pay if your credit or debit cards are stored in the Wallet App. Utilize Apple Cash within Messages to send and receive money from friends/family and make purchases from participating businesses.

Adding your debit, credit, and prepaid cards to your wallet is the first step in setting up Apple Pay.

Add a credit or debit card.

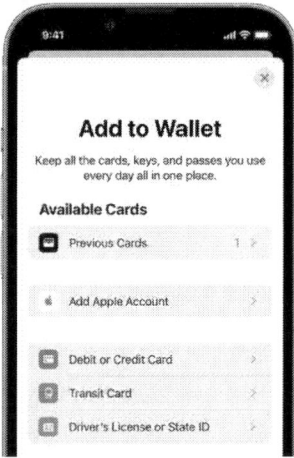

See iPhone: How to Set Up and Use Apple Card for information on how to add Apple Card (the U.S. only).

Follow these steps for all other types of debit and credit cards:

Tap the Add Card button located within a wallet. It is possible that you will be prompted to sign in using your Apple ID.

Choose one of the following options:

1. To add a new card, select Debit or Credit Card from the drop-down menu, then tap Continue. Next, either place your card in the frame so it can be read automatically or manually enter the card's information.

2. Add your previously used cards by selecting Previous Cards from the menu, then selecting a card from the list of cards you have previously employed. These cards could include the card associated with your Apple ID, which you use with Apple Pay on devices other than your iPhone, that you added to AutoFill, or that you removed from AutoFill. Tap the Continue button, authenticate yourself using Touch ID or Face ID, and then enter the CVV number printed on each card's back.

3. If neither of those options works for you, another option is to use the app provided by your bank or card issuer to add your card.

Your card's eligibility for use with Apple Pay is validated by the card issuer, who may contact you for further information to complete the verification process.

Set the default card and rearrange your cards

Your default payment method will always be the card you initially added to your wallet. To make a different card from the active one, move the card you want to use to the top of the stack.

1. Select a card to use as your default in your wallet.

2. To move the card to the top of the stack, touch and hold it with your finger, then drag it forward.

3. To move another card to a different area, tap and hold the card, then drag it to the new spot.

Please consider that Apple Pay and its features may not be available in your nation or region.

PHYSICAL SIM AND E-SIM

> An eSIM is a digital SIM that has become a standard within the industry. With an eSIM, you can activate a cellular plan provided by your carrier without needing to utilize a physical SIM. You can utilize two different phone numbers simultaneously on an iPhone if you install eight or more eSIMs on the device.

Utilize Dual SIM on your Apple iPhone.

The following are examples of devices that support dual SIM:

- iPhone XR, iPhone 11 to iPhone 13, iPhone SE (3rd generation), and iPhone 14 (bought outside of the United States); these devices can use one physical SIM and one eSIM simultaneously.
- Please be aware that the eSIM service is not yet accessible in all countries and areas.
- You can use Dual SIM in many different ways, including the following:
- Assign a specific number to your company calls and a different one to your calls.
- When traveling to a different country or region, sign up for a local data plan.
- Have separate voice and data plans.

Note that your iPhone needs to be unlocked to use with more than one carrier.

Set up Dual SIM

o Navigate to the Settings menu and select Cellular. Next, check that you have at least two active lines (below SIMs). See "Set up cellular service on iPhone" for instructions on how to add a line.

o Activate two lines by tapping one of the lines and then tapping the Turn On this Line button.

o You also can adjust options such as the Cellular Plan Label, Wi-Fi Calling (if your carrier supports it), Calls on Other Devices, and SIM PIN. The label is displayed in the Phone app and Messages and Contacts.

o Select the line you want to use as the default for cellular data by tapping Cellular Data and then tapping a line. You can use either line based on coverage and availability by activating Allow Cellular Data Switching.

o If you have Data Roaming turned on and you go outside of the country or region that is serviced by the carrier's network, you may be subject to additional fees known as roaming costs.

o Select the line that will be used by default for voice calls by tapping the Default Voice Line button, then tapping a line.

Take the following into consideration when utilizing dual SIM:

• Wi-Fi Calling needs to be activated for a line for that line to be able to receive calls even when another line is already being used for a call. Suppose you are receiving a call on one line while the other line is being used for a call, and there is no Wi-Fi connection available. In that case, the iPhone will use the cellular data of the line used for the call to receive the call that is being received on the other line. There may be a fee involved. To receive the call that is being placed to the other line, the line that is currently engaged in a call must have your Cellular Data settings configured so that it is permitted for data use.

• If you do not turn on Wi-Fi Calling for a line, any incoming phone calls on that line (including calls from emergency services) will go directly to voicemail (if available) when the other line is in use, and you will not receive missed call notifications for those calls. This includes calls from emergency services. This applies even if you have emergency services calling you on that line.

You can prevent calls from going to voicemail by contacting your carrier for information on how to set up conditional call forwarding, which allows you to redirect calls from a busy or out-of-service line to another line at a predetermined point in time.

• If you use another device, like a Mac, to make a phone call and then relay it through your iPhone with Dual SIM, the call will be made using the voice line assigned to your default voice line.

• If you begin a conversation via SMS or MMS Messages on one line, you won't be able to switch it to another line until you delete the previous discussion and begin a new one using the other line. If you start the conversation on the first line, you can switch it to the other line at any time. You may be subject to additional costs if you send SMS or MMS attachments on a line that has not been designated for receiving cellular data.

• Both Instant Hotspot and Personal Hotspot use the line chosen for cellular data.'

You can change a physical SIM card to an electronic SIM card on the same iPhone.

If your carrier supports the feature, you can use the same iPhone to convert a physical SIM card to an eSIM. Take the following actions:

1. On your iPhone, go to the Settings menu and select Cellular.

2. Select Convert to eSIM from the menu.

   If you cannot find an option to convert to an eSIM, then your carrier does not allow this feature. You can move your phone number from your traditional SIM card to an eSIM by contacting your carrier or scanning a QR code. This can be done utilizing the eSIM Carrier Activation service.

3. Tap Convert Cellular Plan.

4. Select Convert to eSIM from the menu.

5. Patiently wait for your eSIM to become active. When you activate a cellular plan on your iPhone, your prior SIM card will automatically deactivate.

6. Take out the ejectable SIM card from your iPhone. The next step is to restart your iPhone.

CHAPTER 2:

GET TO KNOW YOUR PHONE

SETTING UP SIRI + HOW TO USE IT

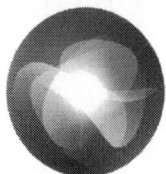

- You can use just your voice to accomplish day-to-day tasks. You can use Siri to translate a phrase, set the alarm, look up a location, report the weather, and do various other tasks.

Voice input is processed on iPhones and other supported devices, but Apple receives transcripts of what users ask Siri to do so that the service can be improved. This information will not be linked to your Apple ID and will only be saved for a predetermined amount of time. You also have the option to turn on the Improve Siri and Dictation feature. If you choose to participate, the audio of your interactions with Siri and Dictation will be sent to Apple so that the company

can help develop and improve Siri, Dictation, and other language processing features such as Translate or Voice Control. This will only happen if you opt-in.

Set up Siri

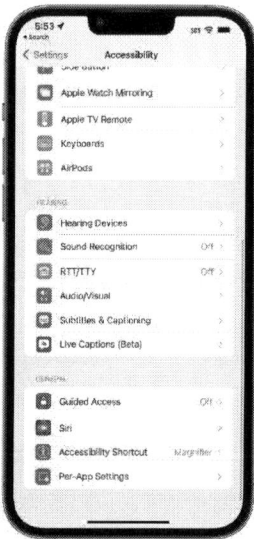

If you haven't activated Siri when you first set up your iPhone, you can do so by navigating to Settings > Siri & Search and then selecting one of the following options:

• To activate Siri using your voice, you will need to turn on the option to Listen for "Hey Siri."

• If you want to activate Siri by pressing a button, you can either turn on the option to press the side button for Siri (on an iPhone with Face ID) or press the home buttonfor Siri (on an iPhone with a Home button).

The following is a list of the actions to take to train Siri to recognize your voice:

1. Open the Settings menu.
2. Tap Siri & Search.
3. Deactivate the Listen for "Hey Siri" setting, then activate it again.
4. When the screen for setting up "Hey Siri" opens, hit the Continue button.
5. Repeat each of the commands displayed on your screen aloud.
6. Tap Done.

Simply using your voice will activate Siri. Siri will give you a verbal response whenever you use your voice to start it.

- Begin by greeting Siri with "Hey Siri," and then proceed to ask a question or make a request.

- Say something to the effect of, "Hey Siri, what's the forecast for today?" as an illustration. Or "Hey Siri, wake me up at eight in the morning."

> ➤ Either repeat the phrase "Hey Siri" or tap the " Siri " button to ask another question or make another request.

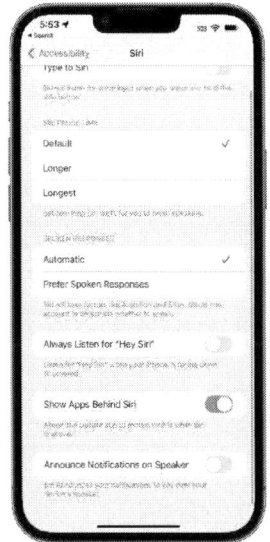

Note: If you want to stop your iPhone from answering when you say "Hey Siri," you may either turn your iPhone over so that the display is facing down or navigate to Settings > Siri & Search and turn off Listen for "Hey Siri."

While wearing AirPods with the appropriate support, you can also activate Siri by saying, "Hey, Siri."

Activate Siri with a button

When you activate Siri with a button when the iPhone is in silent mode, Siri will calmly answer you. You will hear her responses if you turn off Siri's silent mode.

1. Select an action from the list below:

· If you have an iPhone equipped with Face ID, press and hold the button on the side of the device.

· To use the Home button on an iPhone, hold it down until the Home screen appears.

· To use your EarPods, press and hold the button labeled "center" or "call."

· You can start using CarPlay by either touching and holding the Home button on the CarPlay Home Screen or pressing and holding the voice command button on the steering wheel. Either of these actions will allow you to use CarPlay.

· To activate Siri Eyes Free, press and maintain pressure on the voice command button located on your steering wheel.

➢ When Siri appears, you should address her with a question or a request. For instance, you could ask, "Can you set the timer for three minutes."

➢ Tap the Siri icon whenever you want to ask another question or make another request.

Touch-activation of Siri is also available on AirPods with the appropriate software.

Correct if Siri misunderstands you.

• Restate your question by tapping Siri and rephrasing what you want to ask differently.

• Spell out part of your request: You can repeat your request by tapping Siri and then spelling out any terms that Siri didn't comprehend the first time. For instance, after saying "Call," spell out the person's name in full.

• Modify your request by adding text: You can edit it if it is displayed on the screen. Tap the request, and then utilize the keyboard that appears on the screen.

If Siri stops responding

1. Open the Settings menu.

2. Select the Siri & Search option.

3. Tap Siri Responses.

4. Select the Prefer Spoken Responses option to have Siri speak responses even when Silent mode is active on your device.

FAMILIARIZE WITH SAFARI

You could browse the internet, view websites, get a sneak peek at links to other websites, translate webpages, and even restore the Safari app to your home screen if it was accidentally deleted. Using the same Apple ID to sign in to iCloud on multiple devices ensures that your open tabs, bookmarks, history, and Reading List are continuously updated across all devices.

View websites with Safari

A few clicks are all that is required to navigate your way around a webpage.

• Climb your way back to the top: If you want to get back to the top of a long page more quickly, double tap the top border of the screen.

• Look at the rest of this page: Change the orientation of your iPhone to the landscape.

• Reload the page in your browser: Move your cursor down the page from the top.

• Share links: Tap the share button at the bottom of the page.

Installing extensions in the Safari app enables you to tailor the behavior of your browser to your specific needs. Attachments, for instance, can assist you in locating coupon codes when you are shopping, block content on websites, grant you access to features from other apps, and much more.

View and add Safari extensions

1. Select Extensions from the menu after going to Settings > Safari.

2. Select More Extensions from the drop-down menu to go through the available extensions in the App Store.

3. When you locate an application that interests you, tap the price, or if it is free, tap Get, and then follow the instructions on the screen.

Use extensions

Extensions can access the content of the websites that you visit. You can modify the level of access granted to each extension:

1. Start by tapping the left side of the search field, and then tap the extension for which you wish to grant permissions.

2. Determine the level of access granted to each extension.

It is essential that you examine the extensions you have now installed and become familiar with the functions they provide.

Remove an extension

1. Swipe down on the Home Screen, and then look for the extension you want to get rid of.

2. To delete the extension, touch and hold its icon, then tap the Delete app button. Finally, follow the instructions that appear on the screen.

Adjusting Safari's privacy and security settings is possible.

To enable or disable any of the following, navigate to Settings > Safari and look for the section labeled Privacy & Security.

Preventing Tracking on Other Websites Safari's default settings restrict cookies and data collected by other parties. If you want to enable tracking across sites, turn off this option.

Hide your IP address Safari will automatically protect your IP address from being tracked by known websites when you use this feature. When you use Safari to browse the web with an eligible iCloud+ subscription, your IP address will be concealed from trackers and websites you visit. Your IP address will not be concealed if you choose to disable this feature.

Do Not Allow Any Cookies: You can block websites from adding cookies to your iPhone by activating this option and turning it on. (Go to Settings > Safari > Clear

History and Website Data on your iPhone in order to delete any cookies that are already stored on your device.)

Warning About Potentially Phishing Websites If you visit a website that Safari believes may be used for phishing, you will see a warning about it. If you do not wish to be notified about potentially fraudulent websites, you may deactivate this option.

This prohibits websites from viewing your personal information in order to show you targeted advertisements, and it's called privacy-preserving ad measurement.

Check for Apple Pay Websites that accept Apple Pay have the ability to check your device to determine if it has the Apple Pay app installed and enabled. Turning off this option will prevent websites from determining whether or not you have Apple Pay installed on your device.

When you use Safari to visit a website that isn't secure, a warning message will appear in the Safari search field.

APPS: WHICH ONES ARE THE BUILT-IN AND QUICK FAMILIARIZATION.

> The Built-in Apps included are: Camera, Photos, Health, Messages, Phone, FaceTime, Mail, Music, Wallet, Safari, Maps, Siri, Calendar, iTunes Store, App Store, Notes, Contacts, Books, Home, Weather, Reminders, Clock, TV, Stocks, Calculator, Voice Memos, Compass, Podcasts, Watch, Tips, Find My, Settings, Files, Measure, Magnifier, Shortcuts and Translate.

You can locate your apps by using the App Library.

Swipe left from the Home Screen until you reach the App Library on your device. Your apps will be sorted into the appropriate categories automatically. For instance, you might find the apps you use for social networking categorized under the Social heading. The order of the apps in your app drawer will be rearranged itself automatically based on how often you use each app.

Try looking for what you need in the App Library.

Navigate to the Application Library.

After tapping the search area, enter the name of the application that you want to find. Simply tapping on the app will launch it.

Remove an application from your device's App Library.

You may open the list by going to the App Library and tapping the search area there.

Keep your finger on the icon of the app while you do so, and then hit the trash can symbol to delete the app.

Repeat tapping the Delete button to confirm.

You will need to turn off any parental restrictions that are set up on your device before attempting to uninstall an app that was not developed by Apple.

Put applications in the App Library.

To use the app, touch and hold it.

Tap the Remove App button.

Tap the Remove button located on the Home screen.

FAMILIARIZE YOURSELF WITH THE CAMERA AND FEATURES.

The iPhone 14 Pro camera, which has a sensor with 48 megapixels, is the absolute highlight of this article. This makes possible a few things, including:

By default, the camera clusters pixels into groups of four, which results in photographs with a resolution of 12 megapixels and an improvement in lighting

You can take images with the full resolution of 48 megapixels by using the ProRAW format.

There is a new zoom step between the wide angle (1x) and telephoto (3x) positions (by cropping into the new larger sensor for a 2x zoom)

If you leave the iPhone 14 Pro's mode set to be automatic, it will intelligently decide when to go for pixel binning and when to aim for higher-resolution photographs. Once you have ProRAW enabled, you can "force" 48 megapixels, and the phone will still use machine learning and post-processing to give a large, high-resolution image. Once you have ProRAW enabled, you will have this choice.

The 2x step is a cut from the 48 MP sensor, and Apple refers to it as "optical-quality zoom" (yeah, Apple has a propensity for giving things names that make them sound distinctive and original). It is accessible for regular shooting modes and Portrait mode, giving you additional options when it comes to arranging elements inside a scene.

Despite maintaining a resolution of 12 megapixels, the ultra-wide camera has been updated with a larger sensor below. This, together with an aperture of F2.2 and Apple's newly developed Photonic Engine (an improvement to Apple's Deep Fusion, the image-processing algorithm), ensures considerably improved performance in low-light environments. Even in low-light situations, the wide-angle and telephoto cameras appear to generate photographs of far higher quality.

Better Night Mode

The first thing to do is to bin the pixels. In addition to this, Apple improved its Deep Fusion imaging pipeline to something that the company refers to as the Photonic Engine. It takes multiple pictures at different exposures, selects the best-exposed image from each section of the frame, and then combines all those images into a single clear and well-lit picture. This functionality is very similar to that of Google's HDR+.

Selfie camera with auto-focus

Auto-focus and a larger aperture of F1.9 have been added to the front-facing selfie cameras found on both the non-Pro and Pro variants. A wide gap makes it possible for more light to enter the camera, but it also causes more blurring of things that are out of focus, necessitating an auto-focus feature. In comparison, the front cameras of the iPhone 13 series have a fixed focus, and their apertures are set to F2.2.

Action Mode video

Exceptionally stable, allowing for incredibly fluid motion pictures. We presume this will substantially crop the image towards the center, so you should only turn it on when it is essential.

Cinematic mode gets 4K and 24 FPS.

You were previously limited to 1080p at 30 frames per second, but now you can access more options. When editing the film, not only will you have more power over modifying the focus points, but you will also be able to combine clips shot at 24 and 30 frames per second within the same project. Integrated within the iPhone 14 as well as the iPhone 14 Pro.

Adaptive LED flash

Adjusts the power of the flash depending on the camera's focal length, allowing for up to a twofold increase in brightness for telephoto images.

GETTING TO KNOW THE APPLE STORE

Apple Store is the virtual shop where you can download, for free or for a fee, different applications for your phone. If you have an app you would like to download, or more simply just browse around to take a look at what is available:

1. Tap on the App Store logo on your phone

Your first screen that will appear, once you've entered the app, will show you the main and more trending applications of the moment, which could be games, social media, and much more.

On the top right of the corner you will see either a little portrait icon, or your initials. If you tap on it you will be able to take a look at your information. For example, if you are looking for something you've purchased on your old phone, but cannot remember the app's name, simply tap on *Purchased* to have a list of what you have purchased in the past. Another option on this page, that can come in very handy, is the *Subscriptions.* If you have a hard time keeping track of the applications that have a monthly billing and would like to delete some, or perhaps get a better picture of your spendings, by tapping on this option you will be presented with a list of all the applications you have installed that have a monthly fee. By tapping on the specific app you will be able to manage your subscription.

Going back to the main page of the app, we will see at the bottom of the screen different options, *Today, Games, Apps, Update, and Search.*

a. If you tap on *Games* you will be able to take a look on what are the games that are at the top of the charts of the moment.

b. By tapping *App* you will be presented with a list of applications that are more centered in making your daily activities easier, such as: notes, learn applications, and much more.

c. By tapping on *Updates* you will be able to see what applications have been recently updated on your phone, and read more information about it.

d. Lastly, the search icon will allow you to search for a specific application, by simply typing in the search box.

APPLICATIONS: HOW TO DOWNLOAD, UPDATE, UNINSTALL AND MOVE ACROSS YOUR SCREEN.

As we have just went through, the place to go, to get applications is the App Store. Handling your application is quite easy.

To download:

Before downloading, find the application you are looking for. Once you have found it, tap on the "get" button that will appear right next to the application.

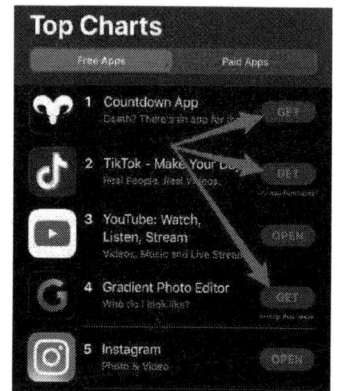

Reminder:

a. If GET appears, the application is free of any charges.

b. If the application requires a payment, the due amount will appear instead of "get"

Once you have tapped on the "get" box and the app was successfully downloaded to your phone it will appear automatically on your screen.

Reminder:

If an icon with a cloud and a narrow pointing down appears next to the application this means that the application was once downloaded on your iPhone or another apple device.

To update your application:

To update any of your application you can open your App Store by searching for the specific application you want to update. *Sometimes a way of saying that an application needs an update is for this one to not function correctly.* Once you have found the application you want to update, tap on the "update" button that appears right next to the App. If the application does not show "Update" but instead "Open", this means that the application has no updates available, or it is up to date.

Another way of finding a list of applications that are available for updates is by simply tapping on the "Update" icon that can be found at the bottom of the App Store page. By following this step you can either choose to update a specific application or update all the application in need of an update, to do so simply tap on "Update All".

To uninstall an application

To uninstall/remove an application from your phone tap and hold down the application. A little panel with several options will appear, select "Remove app". A new series of selection will appear:

a. Delete App: to completely uninstall the application from your phone

b. Remove from Home Screen: this option will simply delete the application from your screen, but the app will remain on your phone. The application can be found again in the app library.

c. Cancel: to cancel.

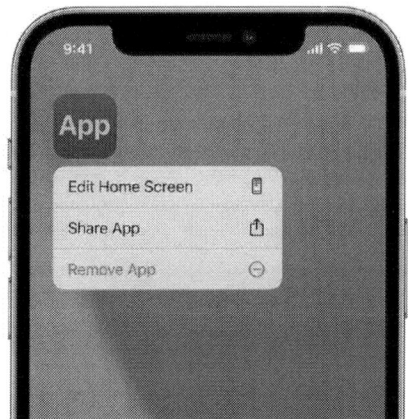

Another simple way to delete an application is to tap and hold the app's icon, keep holding down the icon and slightly move the icon across the screen. This movement will cause the app to shake. To delete the application simply tap on the "-" button that appears at the top left corner of each icon.

To move an application around the screen

If you wish to move your applications around, maybe because you want to reorganize your space better, you can move your application's icons around your screen. To do this, simply tap, hold and slightly move the app across the screen. Once you have done this movement, all the applications' icons will shake. At this point you may choose any app and drag it across the screen until you have reached the desired position.

GESTURES

All of the latest models of iPhones come with no home button, this means that all those commands that we previously did by pressing on the home button have been replaced with gestures and swiping on the screen of your phone. Here are the essential gestures that you should be aware of in order to use your phone.

1. Swiping up from the bottom of your screen to the top and hold: this will allow you to have access to the apps you have currently open. Scroll back and forth between the windows to open the app you want.

2. Swiping up the application cart (step one) + tap on the app page + swipe all the way up the screen: this will allow you to completely close an application.

3. *Swipe left or right on the home screen:* to navigate around the pages of your home screen and have access to all the apps. If you swipe all the way to left you will have access to your widgets. If you swipe all the way to the right you will have access to your app library, where you can see a categorization of your applications as well as the alphabetical list of your application.

4. *Swiping from top to bottom:* to bring out your quick control

6. *Swiping from the top left:* to bring out your notifications

7. *Swiping down from the top right of the screen:* to have access to your control center

CHAPTER 3:
STAYING IN TOUCH WITH THE WORLD

HOW TO ADD NEW CONTACTS TO YOUR IPHONE

1. From the home screen of your iPhone, select the Contacts app icon, which looks like an address book with the shapes of a man and a woman that have been filled in with gray. You also have the option of opening the Phone app, which is denoted by a green icon with a white phone on it, and selecting the Contacts icon, which can be found on the bottom toolbar of the program after you have launched it.

2. Tap the plus sign in ➕ the top right corner of your screen to add a new contact.

3. Enter the person's first and last name, phone number, email address, mailing address, birthday, website URL, and more.

Take note that in order to preserve the contact, at least one of these fields needs to have information entered into it by you. You also have the option of adding a picture by hitting the "add photo" icon that is located in the top left corner of the screen.

HOW TO MAKE AND RECEIVE PHONE CALLS

How To Make A Phone Call

You can initiate a call using the Phone app by dialing a number using the keypad, tapping a recent or favorite call, or selecting a number from your contacts list.

Say "call" or "dial" followed by a number to Siri. Siri will take your call. Pronounce each numeral in turn, for example "four one five, five five five..." You can refer to the 800 area code in the United States by simply saying "eight hundred."

Alternately, try the following:

1. Tap Keypad.

2. Carry out one of the following actions:

   ➤ Use a different line: Tap the line at the top of the screen on models that have a dual SIM slot, then select a line.

   ➤ Input the number using the keypad that is provided: If you make a mistake, you can correct it by clicking the Delete option.

   ➤ Dial the previous number again: You can view the most recent number you dialed by tapping the Contact button, and you can then hit the Call button again to call that number.

   ➤ Put in the number that you copied earlier: After tapping the phone number field located above the keypad, select Paste from the menu.

   ➤ There will now be a brief pause of two seconds: To insert a comma, tap and hold the star (*) key until one appears on the screen.

   ➤ To initiate a hard pause (which will stop the dialing process until you hit the Dial button), enter the following: To produce a semicolon, press and hold the pound (#) key until one appears.

   ➤ To make an international call, press the "+" key: While holding down the "0" key, wait for the "+" symbol to appear.

3. To begin the call, press the Call button on your keyboard.

   ➤ Tap the End Call button to put an end to the current call.

Call Your Favorites

1. To make a call, tap Favorites, then pick one from the list.

  ➤ The iPhone will select the appropriate SIM card for a call in the following order when using a Dual SIM model:

    ○ This contact's chosen method of communication (if set)

    ○ The number that was dialed for the most recent call placed to or received from this contact.

    ○ The voice line that is used by default.

2. Any of the following can be done in order to manage your Favorites list:

    ○ Add a favorite: After tapping the Add button, select a contact from the drop-down menu.

    ○ Rearrange or delete favorites: Tap Edit.

Simply redial the number or give us a call back.

Say something to Siri like, "Redial that last number," or "Return my last call." Siri will respond appropriately.

In addition to that, you could also perform the following:

1. To make a call, tap Recent, then select a contact from the list.

2. Tap the More Info button whenever you want additional information regarding an incoming call or the caller.

   A number of missed calls is displayed in the form of a red badge.

Make a phone call to someone who is on your contacts list.

Siri: Something along the lines of "Call Ara's mobile" should be said.

Alternately, try the following:

1. Tap the Contacts tab within the Phone app.
2. First, select the contact you wish to call, then hit the desired phone number.
   - If you haven't specified a preferred voice line for this contact, the Dual SIM model's default voice line will be utilized for the call even if it has one.

Modify the settings for your outgoing calls.

1. To start, navigate to Settings > Phone.
2. Take one of the following actions:
   - The show must go on. My Caller ID Displays: (GSM) Your telephone number can be found in the "My Number" section. Even if caller ID is off, FaceTime shows your phone number.
   - Dial Assist should be on for all international calls: (GSM) When Dial Assist is activated on an iPhone, the device will automatically insert the appropriate international or local prefix whenever you call one of your contacts or favorites.

HOW TO SEND MESSAGES [Different colors of bubbles]

Send A Message

To initiate a conversation with one or more individuals, you can send a text message to them.

1. To start a new message, hit the Compose button located at the top of the screen. Alternatively, you can tap an existing message.

2. Enter each recipient's phone number, contact name, or

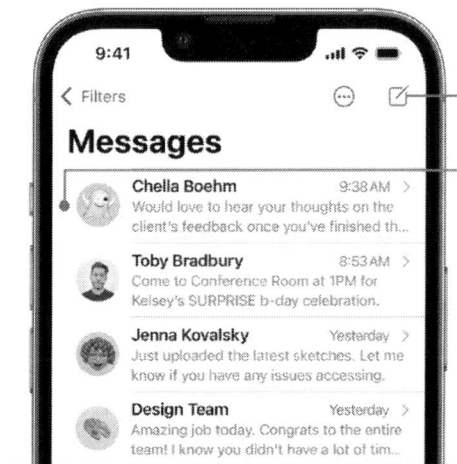

Start a conversation.

A blue dot indicates unread messages.

Apple ID in the appropriate field. Alternately, press the Add button, then select contacts from the drop-down menu.

- If you want to send an SMS or MMS message from a line other than the one that is showing and you have Dual SIM set up on a model that is compatible with it, select the line that is showing, then choose the other line from the drop-down menu that appears.

3. First, tap the text field, then input your message, and last, send it by tapping the Send button.

- If the button to send the message is blue, it indicates that the message will be sent using iMessage. If the button to send the message is green, it indicates that the message will be sent using SMS/MMS or your cellular service.

- If a message cannot be sent, a warning icon will appear on the user's badge. Tap the notification to resend the message to the recipient.

A helpful hint is that you can dictate text by tapping the Dictation button rather than typing each individual letter of your message.

To see the conversation history, simply tap the person's name or phone number that shows at the very top of the screen. If you tap the contact, you will be presented with a number of options, including those to modify the contact card, share your location, see attachments, leave a group conversation, and more.

To exit a discussion and return to the list of messages, either hit the Back button or swipe left from the edge of the screen.

Continue A Conversation

The beginning of a discussion takes place when you receive a message from someone for the first time. If you have previously communicated with that individual in Messages, their message will be appended to the conclusion of the previous thread of discussion.

1. From the Messages list, select the thread of the conversation in which you wish to take part, and tap it.

   - Tap the search field that's located above the Messages listings in order to hunt for contacts and content within chats. (It's possible that you'll need to swipe down in order to access the search area.) Additionally, suggested contacts, links, photographs, and other content are opened when you click on the search area.

2. Select the text field with the mouse, then start typing your message. Tap the Next Keyboard, Emoji button or the Next Keyboard button, and then tap each word that you want to have replaced with an emoji.

3. To send your message, select the Send option from the menu.

You can inform the recipients of your messages that you have read them by going to Settings > Messages and turning on the option to Send Read Receipts.

A helpful hint is to drag the message bubble to the left in order to discover what time a message was delivered or received.

During a discussion, in response to a particular message.
You can respond to a specific message inline to increase clarity and conversation structure.

1. While participating in a chat, touch and hold a message, then tap the button labeled "Reply the Reply."
2. After you have finished writing your response, select the Send option.

A helpful hint: Tapback expression allows you to rapidly respond to communications (for example, a thumbs-up or a heart). To respond to a message bubble, double-tap the bubble and then select the "Tapback" option from the menu.

You may send and receive texts by using siri.

Siri has the capability to read aloud any incoming messages to you, and you may use voice commands to respond to messages that Siri will then send. Educate yourself on how to use Siri.

Siri: Say something like:

- "Send a message to Eliza asking how about tomorrow," the instruction read.

- "Reply that's some really wonderful news."

A helpful hint is that when you are wearing your AirPods, you can still utilize Siri to listen to and answer to messages (2nd generation and later).

You have the option of programming Siri to send a message on your behalf after she has finished reading it to you. Navigate to Settings > Siri & Search > Automatically Send Messages if you wish to eliminate the need to confirm the transmission of messages by going to the Settings menu.

You should communicate with a company.

Some companies give their customers the opportunity to contact with them directly in order to get answers to queries, problems solved, recommendations on what to purchase, the ability to pay with Apple Pay, and other services.

1. Using Maps, Safari, Search, or Siri, look for the company that you wish to interact with and find its location.

2. Begin a chat by clicking on a message link that appears in the search results; the link may take the form of a button, a text link, or the company's logo, among other possible presentations.

On the websites or mobile apps of some businesses, you can send a message directly to the firm.

Note: Messages that are sent to participating businesses show in a dark gray color to differentiate them from messages that have been sent via iMessage (which appear in blue) and SMS/MMS messages (which appear in red) (in green).

Send an audio message that has been recorded.

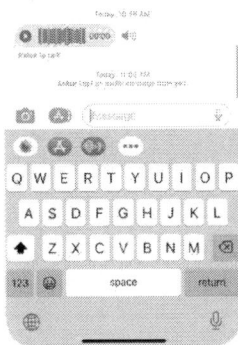

You can rapidly record an audio message that can be played directly within the discussion that you are having in Messages as an alternative to writing a text message.

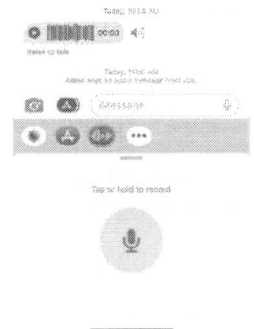

iMessage has an app for recording audio. Tap the Apps button within a discussion in Messages to display the app icons below the text field.

Next, tap the Audio Recording button, and then choose one of the following options:

o To start recording, hit the Record button, then tap it again to stop recording. You can then check what you've recorded before transmitting it. After reviewing the tape by tapping the Play button, you can either transmit it by tapping the Send button or cancel by tapping the Cancel button.

o To speak into a recording device and quickly send the message: Keep your finger on the Record button.

Note that the audio message you send will be removed from the discussion two minutes after it has been sent, unless you hit the Keep button beforehand. Those who have received your recording can still play it. To ensure that your audio messages are kept permanently, navigate to Settings > Messages > Expire (located underneath Audio Messages), then select Never from the drop-down menu.

You can switch to FaceTime instead of sending a message if you would want to make an audio or video call instead. Tap the FaceTime button when you are having a discussion in Messages.

You can either listen to a prerecorded audio message or respond to it.

1. Bring the iPhone up to your ear to listen to incoming voicemails and other audio communications.

2. Bring it up once more for a response.

To activate or deactivate this feature, navigate to Settings > Messages and then activate the Raise to Listen switch.

Text messages can be forwarded to other devices.

When you communicate with someone who uses a device other than an iPhone, the message you send is converted into an SMS and delivered to the recipient. You have the ability to configure your iPhone in such a way that it will notify all of your other devices whenever you send or receive an SMS message.

1. Navigate to Settings > Messages in the menu.

2. Select the Text Message Forwarding option, and then activate any additional devices that you wish to include.

3. If you are not utilizing two-factor authentication, a six-digit activation number will show on your other device. You will need to enter this code on your iPhone, then touch the Allow button.

The Color Text Bubbles app will walk you through changing the colors of your iMessages.

Utilizing an application is highly recommended over any other method for altering the color of the bubbles that appear in iMessage. There are a number of apps out there that perform comparable duties; however, the vast majority of them demand a membership in order to alter the color of the bubble. If you would prefer not pay for one of these applications, Color Text Bubbles in iMessage gives you the ability to alter the color of the bubbles for free; however, you will be need to tolerate some advertisements.

Using the Color Text Bubbles app will allow you to modify the color of your iMessages as follows:

1. Using the iMessage app, download and install the Color Text Bubbles extension.

2. Open the Messages app on your device.

3. To begin a new discussion, either select an ongoing conversation from the drop-down menu or click the icon labeled "New Message."

4. Tap and hold your finger on the row of program icons that is located directly above the keyboard.

5. While maintaining your finger's contact with the screen, swipe to the left until the Color Text Bubble app appears.

6. Tapping on this app will bring up a variety of different bubble styles to choose from.

7. You have the option of selecting a style and message from the list of predefined options, or you may use the Type Custom Message button to compose your own.

8. If the button to Type Custom Message is not present, you can manually bring it up by tapping in the blank spot where it should be.

9. Enter the text that you want to display here.

10. Select the Bubble Color icon from the menu.

11. Select the color you would like for your bubble. Free users can choose from 12 different color options and 12 different grayscale alternatives.

12. Tap Send.

13. You could see an advertisement or be presented with an option to upgrade. After a brief pause, click the X icon to close an advertisement, and then click Later to cancel the offer to upgrade.

14. Tap the arrow that says Send.

15. The text bubble with the custom color you choose has been sent.

How to Make the Color of iMessage Bubbles a Little Bit Darker

It is possible to adjust the hue of blue iMessage bubbles so that they are a darker blue, even if you do not want to install an app. This can be done. However, this will not have any effect on how other people view your messages.

To make iMessage bubbles a darker blue:

1. Open the app that controls the settings.

2. Go to the bottom of the page and tap the Accessibility button.

3. Select Display & Text Size from the menu that appears in the Vision section.

4. Move the toggle switch for the Increase Contrast function to the on position.

5. You should now notice that the blue lettering in your iMessages is a shade darker.

You Can Customize Your iPhone

One method to give your iPhone a more unique feel is to learn how to modify the color of iMessages. Historically, Apple has maintained a high level of control over the customization options available to users. iPhone users have significantly more control over the appearance of their devices because to recent releases of widgets that can be customized. You may now install custom fonts on your iPhone and switch to Dark mode for an entirely new appearance. Both of these features were previously unavailable. On your iPhone, you may personalize the Control Center so that you can easily access the settings that are most important to you.

HOW TO START FAMILY GROUP CHATS

Your personal life as well as your business life can both benefit from the utilization of group chats as a tool. Whether you are organizing a happy hour, a surprise baby shower, or you just want to send your best friends some amusing memes, a group chat is an excellent method to communicate with several people at the same time.

Different kinds of text messages sent to groups

You could encounter the following three varieties of group messages: group iMessages, group MMSs, and group SMSs. The type of group message that is sent is determined automatically by the Messages app based on the user's settings, the network connection, and the carrier plan. Take, for instance:

1. iMessage for groups. Everyone is using an Apple device, iMessage is activated, and all of the text messages are blue in color. Every element of iMessage, including multimedia attachments, message effects, location sharing, and the ability to name groups, is accessible, and anybody may add to or remove members from a group.

2. Form the MMS group. It appears that at least one individual is not using iMessage or an Apple device, as the color of their text messages is green. Everyone can send and receive multimedia attachments, and everyone can view

all of the messages in the group chat. However, the majority of iMessage's features are not available.

3. Texting in a group At least one member of the group has iMessage and MMS disabled, which means they are able to send and receive messages from people outside the group. They are unable to send multimedia attachments, nor are they able to view the responses in the group chat.

iMessage chats in groups

These conversations are depicted as text bubbles in a blue color. They are protected by end-to-end encryption and go through Apple rather than your carrier. Apple is the middleman. Everyone in the group can do the following when using iMessage:

• Send and receive images, videos, and audio messages
• View all of the group's responses
• Send and receive message effects such as drawings, animations, bubble effects, and more
• Provide the group with their current location.
• Provide the group with a name, add or remove members, mute notifications, or leave the group.
• Share their current location with the group.

Send a text message to a group.

1. Launch Messages and then select the Compose button from the menu.

2. To add people from your contacts, either enter their names or hit the Add button and select the Add contact option.

3. Enter your message, then select the envelope icon next to the Send button. Make sure that MMS Messaging is on on your iPhone before attempting to send a group MMS message. You may activate MMS messaging by going to Settings > Messages and turning it on there. In the event that you do not see an option to activate MMS Messaging or Group Messaging, you should get in touch with your carrier to see whether or not your plan enables Group MMS Messaging.

With the release of iOS 15, any photographs, links, and other forms of content that are sent within the context of a group message will be displayed in the Shared with You section of the app that corresponds to that content. Go to the group message, tap the top of the thread, and then switch off Show in Shared with You if you do not want to see the photographs or any of the other content that has been shared with you in Shared with You.

The appearance of group chats will vary, as will the features available to participants, depending on the settings and kinds of phones that individuals use. You also have the option to turn off notifications or exit a group chat entirely if the conversation becomes too much for you to handle. Here's how to accomplish everything on an iPhone, step by step.

The steps to creating a group chat on your iPhone

Check that the iMessage and MMS options under Settings > Messages are both active on your device.

1. Launch the Messages application that is located on your iPhone. It appears to be a white speech bubble contained within a green box.

2. In the upper-right hand corner of the screen, you'll see a button labeled "Compose."

3. In the "To:" field, start typing the names of the people whose participation you want to invite to the group chat. You can also select people from your contacts list by tapping the plus sign (plus) button.

4. After you have finished typing your message, tap the Send icon. It appears to be an arrow pointing in the upward direction.

How to include new participants in a group chat

In order for this to work properly in iMessage group chats, each member of the group must have an iPhone.

1. Launch the Messages app on your device and go to the group conversation to which you wish to add a participant. Tap the names of the participants at the top of the group chat.

2. To open the drop-down menu, tap the arrow that is located next to the names of the persons who are participating in the group chat. After that, tap the Add Contact button.

3. After you have typed in the name of the individual you wish to add, touch the Done button.

On this page, you have the ability to give a group chat a name and designate a photo for it. When you need to check on or send a message to the group chat, you may find it simpler to find if you change the name of the group chat to something specific based on the people that are in it. You may further personalize the group chat by selecting options such as "Roommate Chat" or "Family," or you can even add a photo icon to the conversation.

How to stop receiving notifications inside a group chat.

1. Launch the Messages app on your device, and then navigate to the group chat whose notifications you wish to quiet. To communicate with a specific person in the group chat, tap their name at the top of the screen.

2. Go to the bottom of the page and select Hide Alerts; then, to turn off alerts, hit the toggle on the right side of the page. When it is activated, it will change from red to green.

In the event that you have been joined to a spam group chat, you have the option to either block, mute, or exit the spam group messaging.

How to exit a conversation that is taking place in a group

1. Launch the Messages app on your device and navigate to the group chat that you wish to exit. To communicate with a specific person in the group chat, tap their name at the top of the screen.

2. Select the "Leave" this Conversation option from the drop-down menu. After that, in the confirmation pop-up, you'll need to tap Leave this Conversation one again to finalize your decision.

HOW TO SEND PICTURES AND VIDEOS

You may share films and pictures with your iPhone.

You can share photographs and videos taken using the Photos app through Messages, Mail, and any other apps that you have installed on your device. Photos will even choose the best pictures you've taken at an event and provide suggestions for people you might want to share them with.

Post your pictures and movies here.

• You can share a single photo or video by opening it, tapping ⬆️ the Share icon, and then selecting one of the available sharing options.

• You can share several photographs or videos by tapping the Select button, then tapping the thumbnails of the photos and videos that you wish to share while seeing a screen that contains multiple thumbnails. To share content, first select an option by using the Share icon.

• To share photographs or videos taken during a specific day or month, navigate to the Library, select Days or Months, select the More Options button, then select Share Photos, and finally select a sharing method from the drop-down menu.

When iCloud Photographs is activated, you will have the ability to send a link to several high-quality photos to other people. iCloud links are kept accessible for a period of thirty days, during which time they can be accessed by anyone, and they can be shared using any app, including Messages and Mail.

You also have the option of utilizing Shared Albums in order to transfer photos and videos to particular individuals of your choosing. Please see the article on Using iCloud Shared Albums with Your iPhone.

Please take into consideration that the maximum file size allowed for attachments is set by your service provider. When a Live Photo is shared, it is converted into a still photo for use with devices or services that do not support Live Photos.

Upload pictures using the Sharing Suggestions feature.

Sharing Suggestions will suggest a group of images from an event that you might want to share and, based on the people who are pictured in those photos, it will also suggest others with whom you might want to share those photos. When you share images with other people, they will receive an email with a link to see your photos on iCloud.com. Your collection will remain public for the next thirty days, but you are free to withdraw permission to share it at any moment.

It is necessary to have iCloud Photographs turned on in order to view your Sharing Suggestions, but anybody can view the photos you choose to share with them.

Photos uses the identifications you've set up in the People album to determine who the people are in the photos you've uploaded. See also How to Locate and Recognize People in Photographs. Before you are able to share the images, you will be requested to add that individual as a contact in your People album if they appear in any of the suggested photos and you do not already have one.

- First, tap the For You tab, and then tap one of the photo collections that appears below the Sharing Suggestions section.
- If you wish to get rid of any of the photographs in the collection, tap the Select button.
- After tapping the Next button, select the Share in Messages option.
- Photos encourages you to show the pictures you took to the other people who were there at the same time as you. Press the contact that has been suggested, or tap the Add People button to share with more people.
- To send an email, tap the Send button.

When you have finished sharing your photographs, the receivers will be asked to send you any photographs they have taken at the occasion.

Hit the photo collection you want to remove from the Sharing Suggestions list, then tap the More Options icon, and finally tap the Remove Sharing Suggestion option.

Tap For You, then tap the collection located below iCloud Links to cancel the sharing of a link that you have previously shared. Click the button labeled More Options, then press the Stop Sharing option.

Keeping or sharing a picture or video you get

• When opening an email, click the item to download it if necessary, then click the Share option. Alternately, touch and hold the object and select the sharing or saving option.

• Taken from a text: To share or save a photo or video, tap it in the discussion, then tap the Share button. To save the image or video directly to your Photos library, you may also hit the Save Messages button in the dialogue window for Messages.

• From a link in iCloud: To save the collection directly to your Photos library, tap the Save Messages button in the dialog window for Messages. Open Photos, select For You, and then select the collection under iCloud Links to share. Click More, then select Share.

Creating an email account

You can set up an email account either manually or automatically via the Mail app on your iOS device.

How to create an automatic email account

Mail may set up your email account with just your email address and password if you use an email service like iCloud, Google, or Yahoo. This is how:

1. Select Accounts from the Settings > Mail menu.

2. Select your email provider after tapping Add Account.

3. Type your password and email address.

4. Tap Next if it appears, then wait for Mail to confirm your account.

5. Tap Save if you see Save. If your email provider isn't shown, select Other and manually add your account.

How to manually set up your email account

Make sure you are familiar with your account's email settings if you need to manually configure your email account. You can search them up or contact your email provider if you don't know who they are. then take these actions:

1. Select Accounts from the Settings > Mail menu.

2. Select Other, then Add Mail Account under Add Account.

3. Type in your name, email address, password, and account description.

4. Press Next. Mail will make an effort to locate the email settings and complete the account setup. Tap Done to finish setting up your account if Mail locates your email settings.

Manually enter account settings

You must manually enter your email settings if Mail is unable to locate them. Select Next, then carry out these actions:

1. Decide whether your new account will use POP or IMAP. You should speak with your email provider if you're unsure which option to pick.

2. Fill out the incoming mail server and outgoing mail server fields. Then select Next. Try to look it up if you don't already have it.

3. Tap Save to complete if your email settings are accurate. You will be requested to make changes to the email settings if they are wrong.

Contact your email provider if you are still having trouble setting up your email account or saving your email preferences.

HOW TO SEND EMAIL

Compose and send email messages using the Apple iPhone

1. Tap the Mail Email icon on your Apple iPhone's Home screen.

- To access the App Library if an app isn't present on your Home screen, swipe left.

2. Choose the account inbox, such as Gmail, Yahoo, etc., if prompted.

3. Select the Compose button.

4. Enter the email address in the To field.

- A list of contacts who match the email address may appear as it is being entered and may be chosen at any time.

- Tap the Plus icon Add icon and then choose the contact to add from your contacts.

5. Select a subject from the Subject field.

6. Type a message in the message field.

7. Select the Messages icon under Send.

Send messages with the iPhone's Mail app.

You can compose new messages, send existing ones, and set delivery times for messages from any of your email accounts using the Mail app.

Write an email message

1. Click the button labeled "Compose."

2. Select the email, then start typing your message in the box that appears. Move your finger from letter to letter as you type and only lift it at the conclusion of each word when using an on-screen keyboard.

3. To modify the format, tap the button to expand the toolbar that is located above the keyboard, and then tap the Text Format button.

You have the ability to alter the color as well as the font style of the text, use a style that is bold or italic, add a list that is either bulleted or numbered, and more.

4. To send your email, tap the button labeled "Send."

You may get a reminder if you forget to add an attachment or a recipient you mentioned in your message before sending it. This occurs if you forget that you mentioned them in your message.

Add recipients

1. Select the field labeled To, then type the recipients' names into it.
While you are typing, Mail will make suggestions for persons from your Contacts, including several email addresses for those individuals who have more than one address associated with their Mail account.

You can also access Contacts by tapping the button labeled "Add Contact," then add recipients from within Contacts.

2. To transmit a copy to other individuals, hit the Cc/Bcc field, and then execute one of the following options:

- First, tap the Cc field, and then type the names of the people to whom you will send a copy of the message.
- Navigate to the field labeled "Bcc," then type in the names of the individuals whose addresses you do not want the other recipients to see.

Once you've put in the names of the people you want to send the email to, you can move their names around in the address fields or drag them from one field to another. For instance, if you decide that you do not want the recipients' names to appear, you can drag their names to the Bcc field.

Use Camera to capture an email address

Using the Mail app on your iPhone, you can utilize Live Text to scan an email address that is printed on a business card, poster, or other similar item. This makes it possible for you to start composing emails without having to manually enter an address.

- First, select the recipient's email address in the To field, then press the Scan Email Address button.
- Align the iPhone's screen such that the email address is visible within the camera's viewfinder.
- Tap the "insert" button once the yellow frame has appeared around the text that has been identified.
- A helpful hint is that you can also extract an email address from a picture.

You can use Send Later to schedule an email.

- To send the email, touch and hold the Send button, and then select the time at which you wish to send it.
- Select the Send Later option to view further available choices.
- Send yourself a copy of the message automatically.
- To activate the Always Bcc Myself setting, navigate to Settings > Mail (below Composing).

Send an email using one of your other accounts.

If you have more than one email account, when you send a message, you can choose which one it comes from.

- To edit the Cc/Bcc and From fields in your email draft, tap the corresponding buttons.
- Tap the From field, then select an account from the drop-down menu.

FACETIME

Activate FaceTime

Pick the settings app Settings app from the home screen, then scroll to and select FaceTime, and then select the switch for FaceTime.

Note that in order to use FaceTime, both you and the person you are calling must have an iOS device that is activated for FaceTime and have a data plan that supports the feature.

You may use the Phone app to make a call using FaceTime.

1. From the home screen, choose the Phone app to access the phone's features.

2. Navigate to the Contacts tab, then choose the person you wish to communicate with. Select the Video or Phone icon that is located next to FaceTime in order to make a FaceTime video or voice call.

You can make a FaceTime call by using the FaceTime app on your mobile device.

1. From the home screen, navigate to and select the FaceTime app.

2. Navigate to the call history and locate the desired contact, or select New FaceTime to initiate a new call and then proceed with the on-screen prompts. Simply choose the Create Link option and then proceed with the on-screen instructions to send a FaceTime link to a user with an Android or Windows device.

Attend to a FaceTime call that has just come in.

Choose the path that best suits your needs:

• To accept the call, first select the Accept icon, then choose Join from the menu.

• To decline the call, select the icon labeled "Decline."

Make a call using FaceTime on your Dual SIM device.

When Dual SIM is turned on, calls placed through FaceTime will be routed through the device's default line. To make a change to this, open the FaceTime app on your device and tap the information icon that is located next to the person you want to modify. Choose the default option, and then choose the desired line. When you are done, select the Done button.

Gain access to the FaceTime settings.

To access the FaceTime settings while you are on an active call, pick the information icon that is located next to the person you want to talk to. Choose the path that best suits your needs.

• LIVE CAPTIONS: With Live Captions, it is possible to have the audio from a FaceTime call transcribed. To turn on or off the Live Caption feature, use the switch provided.

• ADD PEOPLE: If you want to include more people in your FaceTime call, go to the Add People menu option and then follow the on-screen instructions.

• Quiet JOIN REQUESTS: During a FaceTime call that is currently in progress, you can silence join requests by toggling the Silence Join Requests switch.

Choose the screen, then choose the one that best suits your needs:

• To mute the sound, click the icon labeled "Mute."

• SHAREPLAY: If you are on an active FaceTime call, you can use SharePlay to stream the display of your phone and share videos, music, and other media from your phone. Follow the on-screen instructions after selecting the SharePlay icon.

• CAPTURE THE CALL: To record a snapshot of your current FaceTime conversation, select the capture icon from the toolbar.

Choose the call window, then pick the desired choice from the drop-down menu:

• SWITCH BETWEEN FRONT & REAR CAMERAS: Choose the icon that looks like a flip camera.

• Include filtering options, stickers, and text: Click the Effects icon, then click the icon you want to use, and then follow the on-screen instructions.

CHAPTER 4

PERSONALIZE YOUR IPHONE

CHANGE THE VOLUME ON YOUR PHONE

You can adjust the volume on your iPhone no matter what you're doing with it—whether you're talking on the phone, watching a movie, or listening to music—by using the buttons on the side of the device. The buttons allow one to adjust the volume of the ringer, alerts, and any other sounds produced by the device. Siri also allows you to adjust the volume by turning it up or down.

Get to the sound settings

- To change the sound settings, choose settings from the home screen. Then go to Sounds & Haptics in the Settings app.

Change how loud it is

o Press the left-side Volume buttons to adjust music or calls.
o The Sounds & Haptics screen is also where you can change the volume. Choose the Volume slider and move it as you like. To change the volume with buttons or not, turn the Change with Buttons switch on or off.

Silent or vibrate mode

To turn iPhone silent, slide the Ring/Silent switch to the left.

Change the sound of an alert

On the Sounds & Haptics screen, scroll to the notification you want and tap it. Then, tap the sound you want. When you're done, click the Back arrow.

Turn on or off keyboard sounds

On the Sounds & Haptics screen, choose Keyboard Feedback and then the on/off switch for the sound.

HOW TO SET DIFFERENT RINGTONES

You can set the default ringtone and give certain people different ringtones. You can also turn off the ringer and use vibrations.

Change the sound and feel of the alarm.

• See How to change the sounds and vibrations on an iPhone.

The iPhone comes with sounds that play when a call comes in. In addition, you can buy more ringtones in the iTunes Store.

Assign a different ringtone to a contact

• Open the app for Contacts.

• Pick a contact, tap Edit, tap Ringtone, and then pick a sound.

Turn on or off the ringer.

Use the Ring/Silent switch to turn on or off the silent mode. Even when silent mode is on, clock alarms still go off.

To temporarily stop calls from coming in, Focus on iPhone can be turned on or set up.

LOCK SCREEN + HOME SCREEN

Change the way your iPhone locks.

You can make your Lock Screen unique by picking a wallpaper, changing the colors and fonts, putting photos in front of the time, and a lot more. You may add news, weather, and calendar widgets to your Lock Screen.

You can make more than one Lock Screen and change from one to the next. Since a Focus can be linked to each Lock Screen, you can change your Focus by using a different Lock Screen.

Tip: Setting up Face ID (on models with Face ID) or Touch ID (on models with Touch ID) first makes it easier to make a custom Lock Screen. See Face ID or Touch ID Setup.

Lock Screen Maker

1. Hold the Lock Screen until the Customize button appears.

If the Customize button doesn't appear, hold the Lock Screen and enter your passcode.

2. Click the "Add New" button. Lock Screen wallpapers appear.

3. Touch one of the backgrounds to make it your Lock Screen.

You can swipe left or right on some wallpapers to try out different color filters, patterns, and fonts that go well together.

4. Tap "Add," and then do one of the following:
- Choose if you want the wallpaper to be used on both the Lock Screen and the Home Screen: Tap Set as Background Pair.
- Change the Home Screen even more: Tap Customize Home Screen. Tap a color to change the wallpaper color, tap the Photo On Rectangle button to use a custom photo, or tap Blur to blur the wallpaper so the apps stand out.

Change the picture on your Lock Screen.

You can move, style, and update a Lock Screen photo.

To reposition your photo, pinch to zoom in, drag it with two fingers, then pinch to zoom out.

Change the look of the picture: Swipe left or right to try out different styles of photos with color filters and fonts that go well together.

To make a multilayered effect, tap the More button at the bottom right, then choose Depth Effect if you have a photo that can have layers, like one with people, pets, or the sky.

Models that can employ the multilayered effect can. You will not be able to use layering if the topic is either too high or too low, or if it covers an excessive amount of the clock.

Tap Browse after selecting Photo Shuffle to see a preview of the photos and adjust the randomization frequency. Set the shuffle frequency by tapping More and then Shuffle Frequency.

Tip: You can also add a photo to your Home Screen and Lock Screen straight from your photo library. Tap Library in the Photos app, choose a picture, and then tap the Share button. Scroll down and choose "Use as Wallpaper." Then tap "Done," and decide if you want it to show up on both your Home Screen and your Lock Screen.

You have the ability to add applications to your Lock Screen.

You can access information such as the weather, how much battery life you have left, or what's coming up on your schedule quickly and easily by adding widgets to your Lock Screen. Widgets may also be used to customize your Lock Screen.

Customize the Lock Screen by pressing and holding it until the Customize button appears, then tapping it.

- Tap the box next to the time to add widgets to your Lock Screen.

- Tap or drag to add the widgets you want.

If you need to make room for a new widget, hit (-).

Switch between Lock Screens

You can make more than one custom Lock Screen and switch between them all day long. If a Lock Screen is linked to a certain Focus, changing from that Lock Screen to a different one will also change your Focus.

1. Hold the Lock Screen until the Customize button appears.

2. Tap the desired Lock Screen.

Change the Lock Screen

- You can change your custom Lock Screen after you've made it.
- Touch and hold the Lock Screen until the Customize button shows up at the bottom of the screen.
- Swipe to the Lock Screen you want to change, then tap the Add New button.

Any of these things:

- Background: Tap Featured, Suggested Photos, or Photo Shuffle, or a top button. See Add a photo to your Lock Screen for instructions.
- Add widgets: Tap the box below the time, and then tap the widgets you want to add.
- Photo Lock Screen styles: Swipe to change the photo's background (Natural, Black & White, Duotone, Color Wash, etc.) and the time font.
- Add a layered effect to a picture on the Lock Screen: Tap the More button in the bottom right corner, then choose Depth Effect (not available for all photos).
- Tap Focus near the wallpaper's bottom, then choose a new Focus.
- To change how the time looks, tap Customize, tap the time, and then tap the Custom Color button. This will let you choose a font, color, and shade.

Note: In Settings, you can also add new wallpaper.

Get rid of a Lock Screen.

You can get rid of Lock Screens you don't need anymore.

Touch the Lock Screen and hold it until the Customize button shows up at the bottom of the screen.

- Swipe to the desired Lock Screen, swipe up, and tap Trash.

SEARCH YOUR IPHONE

Use the iPhone to search The Home Screen or Lock Screen

Live Text lets you search apps, contacts, Mail, Messages, Photos, and photo text. You can also look up information about stocks and currencies and do math, including unit conversions. You can find and open webpages, apps, and images in your photo library, on your system, and on the web. Search gives you a lot of information in a full window that you can scroll through. This information includes contacts, musicians, actors, TV shows, movies, businesses, and sports leagues and teams.

You can choose which apps you want to show up in search results by going to Settings > Siri & Search. Search makes suggestions based on how you use the app, and as you type, the results change.

- Go to Settings > Siri & Search to choose which apps to search in.
- Scroll down, tap on an app, and then turn on or off Show App in Search.

Use an iPhone to search

1. Tap Search on the Home Screen or Lock Screen.

2. Type a search query.

3. Choose one of these:

- Hide the keyboard to see more results on the screen: Choose Search.

- Open a suggested app: Tap it.

- Act right away: You can set a timer, turn on a Focus, use Shazam to find out the name of a song, run any shortcut, and more. Search for the name of an app to see what shortcuts it has, or use the Shortcuts app to make your own.

- Go to a website that was suggested: Tap it.

- Find out more about a suggestion for a search: Tap it, then tap the result you want to open.

- Begin a fresh search: Tap the button that says "Clear Text" in the search field.

Look for in apps

Many apps have a search field or button to find content. You can find a place in Maps.

Tap the search field or the Search button in an app.

Swipe down from the top if you don't see a search field or button.

2. Type what you want to find, then tap Search.

DO NOT DISTURB MODE

Change the settings for "Do not disturb."

You can set a schedule and change other Do Not Disturb settings to help you focus when you don't want to be disturbed.

- Go to Settings > Focus to change the Do Not Disturb settings on your iPhone.
- Tap Do Not Disturb.

You can choose which notifications from people and apps you want to see or not see, link your Lock Screen or Home Screen, set this Focus to turn on automatically, and add Focus filters.

Turn on or off "Do Not Disturb" mode

1. Swipe down from the top right corner of the screen to open the Control Center and quickly turn on "Do Not Disturb." Choose "Focus" and then "Do Not Disturb."
Note: When Do Not Disturb is turned on, calls and alerts will stop.
2. When Do Not Disturb is turned on, the Lock screen, notification bar, and Control Center will all show a Do Not Disturb icon.

DRIVING MODE

When Driving Focus is on, Siri can read your responses so you don't have to glance at your iPhone. Calls only come in when the iPhone is linked to CarPlay, Bluetooth, or a hands-free accessory.

Set a Driving Goal

- Tap Driving after going to Settings > Focus.
- Follow the instructions on the screen to set up things like "Allowed Notifications."

Turn on or off the Driving Focus.

If you have already set up Driving Focus, you can turn it on or off quickly from Control Center:

- Open Control Center.
- To turn Focus on or off, touch and hold it, then tap Driving.
- The Driving icon displays in the status bar, on the Lock Screen, and in Messages when Driving Focus is turned on.
- When someone sends you a message, they will see that you have turned off notifications. If something is urgent, they can still let you know.

Start the Driving Focus on its own.

- Tap Driving after going to Settings > Focus.

- Tap While Driving under Automatically turn on, and then choose one of the following:

- Driving will start automatically when movement is sensed.

- When connected to car Bluetooth, Driving is activated.

- Driving can be turned on or off manually from the Control Center.

- Activate with CarPlay: When your iPhone is connected to CarPlay, Driving will be turned on by itself.

Change how you get notified.

- To let notifications from certain people through or stop them:

- Tap Driving after going to Settings > Focus.

- Tap People under "Allowed Notifications."

- Touch Allow Notifications From or Silence Notifications From.

- Tap "Add People," then choose the contacts whose notifications you want to let through or turn off.

Share your Focus status

When you enable Driving Focus, apps will show that your notifications are off when others message you. Apps only know that you've turned off notifications, but they don't know which Focus you're using, so the name is never shared. Focus status is shared between apps when you have Focus on and give permission to an app.

Go to Settings > Focus. To turn on Focus status, do the following.

- Click on Focus Status.

- Change Driving to On.

CONTROL CENTER

Control Center gives you quick access to useful settings and apps on your iPhone, like airplane mode, Do Not Disturb, a flashlight, the volume, and the brightness of your screen.

Open the Control Center:

- On an iPhone with Face ID: Swipe down from the right edge of the screen. Swipe up to close Control Center.
- Swipe up on a Home-button iPhone. To close Control Center, swipe down or tap Home.

Use Control Center to get to more controls.

Many controls give you more choices. Touch and hold a control to see what choices you have. For example, in Control Center, you can do the following:

- Touch and hold the group of controls in the top left corner, then tap the AirDrop button to bring up the AirDrop options.
- To take a selfie, take a picture, or record a video, touch and hold the Camera button.

Set up and add controls

You can change Control Center by adding more controls and shortcuts to apps like Calculator, Notes, Voice Memos, and more.

- Click Settings and then Control Center.
- Tap the (+) or (-) button next to a control to add or remove it.
- Touch the Reorder button next to a control, then drag it to a new place.

Disconnect from a Wi-Fi network for a short time

- Tap the Wi-Fi Switch button in Control Center. Tap it again to connect.
- Touch and hold the Wi-Fi Switch button to see the name of the connected Wi-Fi network.
- Because Wi-Fi doesn't turn off when you leave a network, AirPlay and AirDrop still work, and when you move or restart your iPhone, it connects to known networks. Go to Settings > Wi-Fi to turn off Wi-Fi. Tap the Wi-Fi Switch button in Control Center to turn Wi-Fi back on.

Disconnect from Bluetooth devices for a while

- Tap the Bluetooth Switch button in Control Center. Tap it again to allow connections.
- Because Bluetooth doesn't turn off when you disconnect from a device, you can still use location services and other features. Go to Settings, then Bluetooth, and turn off Bluetooth to turn off Bluetooth. Tap the Bluetooth Switch button in Control Center to turn Bluetooth back on.

Turn off Control Center access in apps

Go to Settings > Control Center > Access Within Apps and turn it off.

NOTIFICATIONS

iPhone users can see and respond to alerts

Notifications let you know what's new, like if you missed a call or if the date of an event changed, among other things. You can change your settings for alerts so that you only see what's important to you.

Unless you use Focus to turn off notifications, iPhone shows them as they come in. They roll in from the bottom of the screen to keep you from being too distracted. You can see them in a list view, a stacked view, or a count view on the Lock Screen. To change the layout of the notifications on the Lock Screen, pinch them.

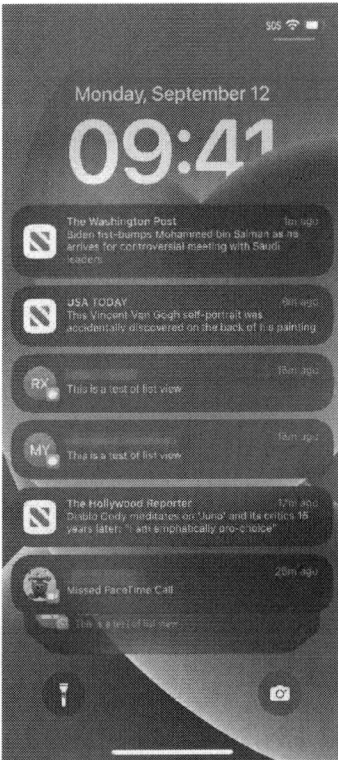

When using an app, you may be asked if you want notifications immediately, never, or at a certain time. Settings > Notifications can change this setting.

Notification Center is where you can find your alerts.

Do any of the following to see your alerts in Notification Center:
- Swipe up from the middle of the screen on the Lock Screen.
- Swipe down from the middle of the top screen on the other screens. After that, if there are any notifications from a previous time period, you can scroll up to view them.
- To close Notification Center, swipe up or press Home.

Response to messages

Multiple Notification Center or Lock Screen notifications are grouped by app, making them easier to see and manage. Notifications from some apps can also be put together using the app's own organization tools, such as putting them together by topic or thread. Notifications that are grouped together look like small stacks, with the most recent one on top.

Any of these things:
- To expand a group of notifications so that you can see each one separately: Tap the bunch. Tap Show Less to get rid of the group.
- To see a notification and take quick actions if the app supports them (on supported models), do the following: Touch the alert and hold it.
- To open the app that sent you a notification, tap the notification.

Set up a reminder summary

- You can make your day less distracting by setting up your notifications to come as a summary. You can choose which notifications to include in the summary and when you want to get it.

- The summary of notifications is tailored to you and sorted by priority based on what you're doing right now, with the most important ones at the top. The summary is especially helpful because it lets you respond to notifications when it's convenient for you. Focus filters notifications while you're focused on an activity.

- To turn on Scheduled Summary, go to Settings > Notifications > Scheduled Summary.

- Choose the apps you want to talk about in your summary.

- Plan how long your summary will be. Tap Add Summary if you want to get another summary.

Notifications can be seen, turned off, cleared, and muted.

When your iPhone alerts you to something, you can do any of the following:

- What to do when you get a notification in another app: Tap on it to see it, and swipe up to get rid of it.

- To clear notifications, swipe left on a notification or a group of notifications and then tap Clear or Clear All.

- Swipe left on a notice or set of alerts, select Options, and then tap either an hour or a day to adjust the time at which the notifications are displayed. This sends them straight to the Notification Center and stops them from showing up on the Lock Screen, making a sound, making the screen light up, or showing a banner.

- Swipe left on a notice or set of notifications, hit Options, and then tap an hour or a day.

- To turn off notifications for an app or group of apps, swipe left on the app or group of apps, tap Options, and then tap Turn Off.

- To change how an app shows notifications, swipe left on a notification, tap Options, and then tap View Settings. See Change the settings for notifications to find out what settings you can change.

- To clear Notification Center, tap Clear Notifications, then Clear.

- Turn on "Do Not Disturb" to stop all alerts from going off. See Focus on iPhone can be turned on or set up.

- If you haven't used an app recently, it may suggest turning off notifications.

Display the most recent messages on the Lock Screen

On the Lock Screen, you can let people use the Notification Center.

- Go to Settings > Face ID & Passcode or Touch ID & Passcode on an iPhone with Face ID.

- Enter your passcode.

- Scroll down and click on Notification Center (below Allow Access When Locked).

PERSONALIZED WALLPAPER

Change your Lock Screen or Home Screen background.

- Tap Wallpaper in the Settings app.

- Click on "Add New Wallpaper."

You can choose your own photo by tapping Photos, People, or Photo Shuffle. You can also choose a wallpaper from a category, such as Weather & Astronomy, Emoji, Collections, or Color.

- You can make more changes to your wallpaper if you want to. Tap Add then.

- You can change your background on the Lock Screen.

Make sure that Face ID has already been set up on your iPhone. Face ID must be able to see your eyes and the area around them in order for you to change your wallpaper from the Lock Screen.

- To get to your wallpaper gallery, touch and hold your Lock Screen.

- Swipe left and right to choose a background you've already made. Tap the Add button to add a new background.

You can also link a Focus to a specific wallpaper by tapping the Focus button, change existing wallpapers, or swipe up on a wallpaper and tap it to delete it.

- Filters, widgets, and styles can be used to change a Lock Screen wallpaper.

- Tap Wallpaper in the Settings app.

- Tap Customize under the picture of your Lock Screen.

- Choose a wallpaper by tapping Customize Current Wallpaper or Add New Wallpaper.

- Make any changes you want to the wallpaper before you tap Done.

- Tap on the time to choose a font and color for the text.

- Tap the boxes above or below the time to add or remove widgets like Calendar, Clock, Weather, Fitness, or Reminders.

- Swipe left or right to use styles like Black & White, Duotone, or Color Wash.

- Pinch and drag your picture to crop and move it.

- Tap the More button to choose a background. When you tilt your screen, Perspective Zoom changes the background. Depth Effect lets you add more than one layer to the subject of your photo.

FONT SIZES

- If you suffer from colorblindness or have any other kind of vision problem, you can adjust the settings of the display so that the screen is easier to see for you.
- Use screen adjustments. Go to Settings > Accessibility > Display & Text Size.

Any of the following can be changed:

- Bold Text: Show the text with characters that are in boldface.
- To make the text bigger, turn on Larger Accessibility Sizes and then use the Font Size slider to change the size of the text.
- This setting changes the size of text in apps that support Dynamic Type, like Settings, Calendar, Contacts, Mail, Messages, and Notes, to the size you want.
- Button Shapes: This setting makes text that you can tap stand out.
- On/Off Labels: This setting shows "1" for switches that are turned on and "0" for switches that are turned off.
- Reduce Transparency: This setting makes some backgrounds less clear and blurry.
- Increase Contrast: This setting changes the colors and text styles to make the contrast and readability better.

- Apps that support Dynamic Type, like Settings, Calendar, Contacts, Mail, Messages, and Notes, change the size of the text to match your preference.
- Differentiate Without Color: This setting replaces user interface elements that use color to show information with alternatives.
- Smart Invert or Classic Invert: Smart Invert Colors swaps the colors on the screen, except for images, media, and some apps that use dark color styles.
- Tap on a color filter to use it. To change the brightness or color, move the sliders.
- Reduce White Point: This setting makes bright colors less intense.
- Auto-Brightness: This setting uses the built-in ambient light sensor to automatically adjust the screen brightness to the current lighting conditions.

When using an app, you can change the size of the text.

- Open Control Center and then tap the Text Size button.
- If you don't see the Text Size button in Control Center, you can add it by going to Settings > Control Center > Text Size.
- Move the slider up or down to change the size of the text.
- Tap All Apps at the bottom of the screen to change the text size for all apps.

DARK MODE

Use Settings or Control Center to turn on Dark Mode.

    1. Go to Settings and then tap Display & Brightness.

    2. Choose Dark to activate Dark Mode.

To turn on or off Dark Mode in Control Center, do the following:

1. Go to Settings, then tap Control Center.

2. Tap the "Add" button next to "Dark Mode" to add it to the Control Center.

Make Dark Mode turn on by itself.

1. Go to Settings and then tap Display & Brightness.

2. Select Automatic.

3. Tap Options to set when Dark Mode will be on.

BATTERY SAVING MODE

Simply navigate to the "Settings" menu on your device and select "Battery" to activate or deactivate the "Low Power Mode.. The Low Power Mode can also be activated and deactivated through the Control Center. You can add Low Power Mode to Control Center by going to Settings > Control Center > Customize Controls, then selecting Low Power Mode from the list of available controls.

When Low Power Mode is on, your iPhone or iPad will last longer before you need to charge it, but some features might take longer to update or finish. Also, you might not be able to do some things until you turn off Low Power Mode or charge your iPhone or iPad to 80% or more.

These features are lessened or changed by Low Power Mode:
- Auto-Lock
- Brightness of the screen
- iPhone and iPad models with ProMotion displays can only have a refresh rate of up to 60 Hz.
- Some things you can see
- iCloud Photos (temporarily paused)
- Auto-downloading
- Get emails • Refresh apps in the background

The battery in the status bar will be yellow when Low Power Mode is on. You'll see a yellow battery icon and how much power is left in the battery. When your iPhone or iPad is charged to 80% or more, Low Power Mode turns off by itself.

CHAPTER 5:

EXTRA TOOLS AND TRICKS

LEARN HOW TO USE BLUETOOTH

You can stream music and videos, make phone calls, and more by pairing your iPhone or iPad with Bluetooth accessories.

On your device, turn on Bluetooth.

Depending on the apps you're using, you might get a warning that says you need to turn on Bluetooth before you can pair an accessory with Bluetooth.

• Tap Bluetooth after going to Settings > Privacy & Security.

• Make sure Bluetooth is turned on for the apps you want to use.

Establish a connection between your device and a Bluetooth accessory.

1. To activate Bluetooth on your device, navigate to the Settings menu, then select Bluetooth. Continue to remain on this screen until all of the steps necessary to pair your item have been completed.

2. Put your attachment into the discovery mode, and then wait for it to appear on the device you're using. Check the instructions that came with your accessory or get in touch with the manufacturer if you can't find it or aren't sure how to make it discoverable.

3. When the name of your item displays on-screen, tap it to begin the pairing process. There is a possibility that you will be required to enter the PIN or passcode. Check the documentation that came with your accessory if you are unsure of your personal identification number (PIN) or passcode.

4. You will be able to use your attachment with your device once it has been paired successfully. Simply repeat these procedures in order to pair multiple Bluetooth items. If you have more than one Bluetooth device associated with your iPhone or iPad, you will have the option to select which one will serve as your primary source of audio.

Remove a pairing from a Bluetooth accessory.

You can disconnect a Bluetooth accessory by going to Settings > Bluetooth, finding the device you want to disconnect, tapping the More Info button, and then tapping the Forget this Device button. This takes the accessory off of the list of Bluetooth devices that are currently available.

You will need to put your device back into discovery mode and go through the pairing process once more before you can reconnect the Bluetooth accessory to your device.

AIRPLANE MODE

While you're flying in an airplane, you can prevent your device from transmitting wireless signals by activating a mode called "Airplane Mode."

Put the device into airplane mode.

Launch Control Center on your iPhone, iPod touch, or iPad, and then hit the Airplane Mode button or the icon for the Airplane Mode button on your iPhone. You may also activate it by going to Settings and choosing the Airplane Mode option there.

You may activate the airplane mode on your Apple Watch by touching and holding the bottom of the screen until the Control Center appears, then swiping up and tapping the Airplane Mode Button Watch Airplane Mode icon. You also have the option to go to Settings and select the Airplane Mode option there.

You have the option of configuring your iPhone and Apple Watch to behave identically to one another when in Airplane Mode. Start by opening the Watch app on your iPhone, then navigate to the General menu, then hit Airplane Mode, and finally select Mirror iPhone.

When you activate the Airplane Mode, all radios, with the exception of Bluetooth, are turned off. Your device will remember that you turned off Bluetooth while it was in Airplane Mode the next time you turn on Airplane Mode if you do so while it was in Airplane Mode the first time.

While in airplane mode, you can still use Wi-Fi and Bluetooth.

You are able to use Wi-Fi and Bluetooth devices even when you are in Airplane Mode if the airline permits it. You simply need to switch each one on independently.

If you're reading this on an iPhone, iPad, or iPod touch:

1. Launch Control Center by tapping its icon on the Home screen.
2. Tap the icon that corresponds to either Wi-Fi or Bluetooth.
3. You also have the option to go to Settings and select Wi-Fi or Settings and select Bluetooth.

When you look at your Apple Watch:

1. To access the Control Center and configure your Wi-Fi settings, touch and hold the bottom of the screen.

2. Swipe up and tap the Wi-Fi icon to connect to the network.

3. You also have the option to navigate to Settings > Wi-Fi. To access Bluetooth, select Settings > Bluetooth from the menu.

If you activate Wi-Fi or Bluetooth while your device is in Airplane Mode, it will remain activated the next time you use Airplane Mode unless you deactivate the features while your device is in Airplane Mode.

HEALTH APLICATION

The Health app was developed to assist in the organization of your vital health information and to make it simple to retrieve from a consolidated and protected location. iOS 16 introduces a new way to manage, understand, and keep track of your medications, as well as significant updates to the Sleep app.

Your medical records, medications, lab results, activity levels, and sleep patterns are just some of the important data that can be accessed through the Health app. And makes it easy to share that information while maintaining its safety.

It gathers health and fitness data from your iPhone, Apple Watch, third-party devices, and HealthKit apps.

The Health app is designed to preserve the confidentiality of your data and guard your privacy. Your data is encrypted, and you have complete authority over the information pertaining to your health at all times.

A wonderful perspective on you.

Machine learning is performed locally on the device in order to provide you with information that is most pertinent to you, such as your steps, sleep, or vitals.

Always be aware of the latest trends.

You are able to examine how important health measurements like blood glucose, heart rate, and respiratory rate vary over time with the use of advanced trend analysis. In addition, you are able to receive notifications if new patterns are identified.

More applications. Extra details are needed.

The Health app is able to include data from tens of thousands of other apps developed by third parties that are intended to promote healthy behaviors. These apps cover a wide range of topics, including fitness, diet, and meditation.

Medication management made simpler.

You can get information on the medications you're taking, as well as alerts about potentially dangerous drug interactions.

- To add a drug to the Health app, you simply need to point your camera at the label of the medication, or you can start typing the prescription's name to view a list of choices.

Forget about forgetting.

You may set alerts on your iPhone or get notifications on your Apple Watch to remind you to log your drugs, vitamins, and supplements. And ensure the safety of your loved ones by sharing information about your medicine with them.

Having control over your sleep is a pipe dream.

Make getting enough rest a top priority by controlling when you go to bed, what you do in the hour leading up to bed, and how often you achieve the number of hours of sleep you need.

Take a look at your sleeping metrics.

Apple Watch monitors various aspects of sleep, including the amount of time spent asleep, blood oxygen levels, heart rate, and breathing rate when sleeping. 3 In iOS 16, the Health app now includes comparison charts that enable you view your heart rate and sleeping respiratory rate in addition to the amount of time you spent sleeping.

Get insights on sleep stages.

With the help of Apple Watch's built-in sensors, you'll be able to gain a more in-depth understanding of how much time you spend in each of the following three stages of sleep: REM, Core, and Deep.

Significant advances in mobility.

Your activity levels can be analyzed using data from your iPhone and Apple Watch. Even if you're walking stability is low or extremely poor and you are at an elevated danger of falling, you can set up the watch to send you an alert.

Keep your rhythm in check at all times.

You are able to log your period, record symptoms such as cramps, and track cycle factors such as lactation with the help of Cycle Tracking. Additionally, it can assist in determining when the beginning of your subsequent period or fertile window will be. You also have the option to receive a notification in the event that your cycle history reveals a potential cycle deviation, such as periods that are irregular or infrequent.

NOTES

Make a brand new note.

1. Open Notes.

2. Create your note by tapping the Compose button, then navigating back to step 1.

3. Tap Done.

The note's title is taken from the first line of the note. To modify the way, the first line of a new note is formatted, navigate to Settings > Notes > New Notes Start with, then choose one of the available options.

Additionally, Notes can be quickly accessed from the Control Center. You can add Notes by going to Settings > Control Center on your device. Then launch Control Center, and after tapping Notes, jot down your thoughts. Alternatively, you could just ask Siri to "Start a new note."

You can do even more with Notes.

You can pin your most important notes, draw, make checklists, scan and sign documents, and add attachments, such as pictures, videos, or links to websites, with the Notes app.

You can make it simpler to find your most important or favorite notes by using the "PIN A NOTE" feature. Swipe right over a note, then let go of the note when you are finished. You could also navigate to the note, tap the More button, then tap the Pin button, and finally tap the Yellow pin button. Swipe right again over a pinned note to remove it from your list of favorites.

TO FORMAT A NOTE: When you are inside of a note, tap the table button that is next to the icon for formatting a table. or the formatting button Formatting icon for titles and headings in the Notes app, if you want to add a table, title, heading, or bulleted list. To quickly open a list of formatting options in the Notes app, you can also touch and hold the Formatting icon for titles and headings. This will bring up the option menu.

TO ADD AN ATTACHMENT: Click the share button in that app. this lets you add from another app. tap notes, then the note you wish to attach something to, and then save

ADD A PHOTO OR VIDEO: To add a photo or video, tap in a note, then tap the Camera button. After that, you will be able to add the photo or video. Use the Take Photo or Video or Choose Photo or Video buttons to create a new photo or video, respectively, or to add an existing one. Tap the Use Photo or Use Video option, or tap the Add button to add one that's already been taken. There is also the option to scan documents and include them in your notes.

Create folders

1. If you are in the Notes list, tap the back arrow icon, which is represented by a yellow arrow, to return to the screen you were on before. to view the list of your folders.
2. From the list of folders, select the New Folder button and then select the New folder icon.
3. Select the location where you want to add the folder. Simply by dragging the folder that you want to have as a subdirectory into the main folder, you may make a subfolder. It will be indented and moved below the main folder in the hierarchy.
4. Give your folder a name, and then hit the Save button.

Transfer a note to a distinct file folder.

1. To return to the screen you were on before entering a note, tap the back arrow icon, which is represented by a yellow arrow. to return to the list of notes you have.
2. To select notes, go to the Notes list, tap the More button, then tap the Select Notes button.
3. Tap the notes that you want to move around in the arrangement.
4. Tap the Move button, then choose the folder you would like to place them in.

See your notes in Gallery view

You now have a new way to view your notes in Gallery view, which makes it much simpler than ever before to locate the specific note you're looking for. Launch a folder or list of notes, navigate to the More menu, and then select View as Gallery from the drop-down menu.

To organize your notes within folders as follows:

1. Proceed to the folder in which you wish to arrange the files.
2. After tapping the More button, select Sort Notes By from the menu that appears.
3. You get to decide how your notes will be organized.
4. You may automatically sort all of your notes by going to Settings > Notes and tapping the Sort Notes By button there. The next step is to decide how you want to organize your notes.

Look for a note or an attachment, if you can.

- To hunt for a particular note, you need only press the Search field, then type in the name of the note you want to find. You have the option of searching for typed notes as well as handwritten ones. Search is able to decipher what's depicted in the photographs contained within your notes. For instance, if you search for "bike," the search engine will display all of the pictures that you've taken that include a bike. Search is also able to locate specific text contained within scanned documents or photos, such as invoices or receipts.

- To look for something in a particular note, you must first choose the note, then click the More button, then select Find in Note, and then key in the information that you are looking for.

- You also have the option of searching for attachments. Press the More button while you are in a Notes list, and then tap the View Attachments option that appears. Simply press and hold the attachment's thumbnail, then select the Show in Note option to navigate to the note that contains the attachment.

Make a note right away from the screen that locks your device.

If you have an iPad that is compatible with Apple Pencil, you can use it to start a new note right from the Lock Screen, or you can continue working on the note you were working on before. You may adjust these settings by navigating to Settings > Notes, tapping Access Notes from the Lock Screen, and selecting an option from the drop-down menu that appears.

Create your message by using the Apple Pencil to tap the Lock Screen on your device. Everything you make is going to be saved in the Notes folder automatically.

IPHONE 14 SENIORS GUIDE

Make sure that your notes are safe.

You have the ability to safeguard any note within the Notes app by encrypting it and making it inaccessible to anyone else who might use your smartphone. Depending on the type of device you have, you may be able to lock and unlock your notes via either Face ID or Touch ID in addition to a password.

Delete a note

1. Swipe left when the Notes list is over the note you want to delete.
2. Make a selection and then press the Trash button.
3. You also have the option to open the note, select the More button, and then select the Delete button.

To retrieve a note that has been deleted, navigate to the Folders list and select the Recently Deleted option. Tap the note that you would like to keep, then tap anywhere within the note, and then tap the Recover button.

Notes can be configured via iCloud.

You can keep your notes up to date across all of your devices by using iCloud Notes. To begin configuring Notes with iCloud, navigate to Settings > [your name] > iCloud, and then toggle the Notes switch to the on position. If you are signed in with the same Apple ID on all of your Apple devices, your notes will show up on all of them.

REMINDER

Create a reminder

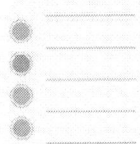

1. Launch the app called "Reminders."

2. Select the "+ New Reminder" option, then begin entering your reminder.

Set a due date

To assign a specific date and time for the reminder, tap the icon labeled Date and Time. You have the option of selecting Today, Tomorrow, or This Weekend, or you can press Date & Time to pick the day and time yourself.

When you create a reminder, if you don't also specify a time for the notification to appear, it will appear at 9:00 AM as the default setting. Launch the Settings app, then select the Reminders option from the menu that appears. This will allow you to adjust the time that all-day reminder notifications display. Simply tap the time that appears below the All-Day Reminders heading, and then select a new time.

Include a location here.

Simply tap the Location button to set a notice that is based on your current location. Choose one of the possibilities that are available, or choose Custom to add your own place. Then, decide whether you want to be told when you are arriving or leaving, and set the boundary of the area that will serve as a reminder for you.

Make sure that the Location Services toggle is set on so that you can receive notifications based on your current location. Launch the Settings app, navigate to the Privacy menu, and then select Location Services to activate the feature.

Add a tag

To add a tag, use the button labeled "Tag." You can quickly and automatically categorize your reminders using tags depending on the keywords you choose. Find out more about how you may arrange your reminders by using tags.

Flag a reminder

By tapping the Flag button, you can highlight a reminder as being of utmost significance and cause it to be displayed in the Flagged smart list on the main screen of the Reminders app.

Add an attachment

To add a photo or other attachment to the reminder, tap the Photos button. You have the option of taking a fresh photo, selecting an image from the collection of images on your device, or scanning a document.

Edit a reminder

If you want to add more information or make changes to your reminder, such as notes, a URL, or a priority, tap the button that says "Edit Details." You are also able to adjust the list that the reminder is part of and modify the notification settings that it uses.

While you are messaging someone, you can get a reminder.

1. Select an item to be reminded about, and then select the Edit Details button.
2. Activate the When Messaging setting.
3. After tapping Choose Person, select a contact by tapping their name.

Create subtasks

You are free to include subtasks in each reminder that you make. A reminder to pack for a trip, for instance, can contain a rundown of items that are particularly important not to leave behind.

There are a number distinct approaches you might use to the creation of subtasks:

- To combine two reminders, tap and hold on one of them, then drag it onto the other reminder. The reminder that you dragged into the other task causes it to become a subtask.

- To indent a reminder, swipe right on it, and then hit the Indent button. The task that is above the reminder is elevated to the status of a subtask. To undo this, slide right once more and then hit the Outdent button on the subtask.

- First select the reminder you want to edit, then touch the Edit Details button. Tap the Subtasks tab, then tap the Add Reminder button, and then type in your subtask. Repeat this process for each additional subtask that you wish to create.

IPHONE 14 SENIORS GUIDE

To complete a reminder, tap the circle that is empty next to it.

This will mark the reminder as having been finished. Tap the More button, then tap Show Completed, to view the reminders that you have already dealt with.

- Swipe left on the reminder, then tap the Delete button to remove it from your list without first marking it as finished.

- Swipe left over the reminder that appears on the Lock Screen if you receive a notification about a reminder. Select View, then select the Mark as Completed option.

Siri can help you set a reminder for it.

You can use Siri on your iOS device or your Apple Watch to set a reminder for you if you simply ask her to do so. The following are some examples:

- "Remind me to give the dog his breakfast at 7:30 a.m. every day," the owner requested.
- "Remind me to check the mail when I get home," the utterance began.
- "Remember to remind me to stop by the grocery store when I leave here," the person said.
- "At three o'clock in the afternoon on Monday, please remind me to call Tara."

If you want Siri to be able to assist you in setting location-based reminders, add both your home and work addresses to your card in Contacts. Launch the Contacts app, then select My Card from the menu. Tap the Edit button, enter your address for either work or home, and then tap the Done button.

You can add a reminder from a different app here.

If you want to be reminded to go back to another app, such as to revisit a website or a location on a map, add a link in your reminder that takes you to the place where you last left off. Launch the application from which you wish to obtain the information again, and then locate the Share button. Tap the icon that looks like a reminder, then.

IPHONE 14 SENIORS GUIDE

ALARM CLOCK

Establish a reminder on your iPhone.

You can schedule alarms in the Clock app for any time of the day, and you can choose to have them recur on one, two, or all seven days of the week.

Say something to Siri like, "Set an alarm for seven in the morning." Educate yourself on how to use Siri.

Note that in addition to configuring a wake-up alarm as part of a full sleep schedule (including bedtimes, wake-up times, and other details), you can do so in the Health app. You can use Clock to establish a regular alarm for the time that you want to wake up even if you do not want to establish a sleep schedule for yourself.

Set a regular alarm

Regular alarms can be set for any time, including the time that you want to wake up, and they can be set on your smartphone. A consistent alarm does not relate in any way to a particular sleeping pattern.

1. Select Alarm from the menu, then select the Add button.

2. After you have established the time, pick one of the following options:

- This must be repeated: pick the days of the week.

- Label: Give the alarm a name, such as "Water the plants," and press the "Label" button.

- Sound: You can select a song, a vibration, or a ringtone.

- Hit the snooze button and allow yourself a few extra minutes of rest.

3. Tap Save.

Put an everyday alarm off its hook.

- To set the alarm, tap the button that is located next to the time.
- To modify the alarm settings, hit Edit in the upper left corner of the screen, and then tap the alarm time.

Remove a regular alarm

- Hit Edit in the top left corner of the Clock app, then tap the Delete button, and finally tap Delete to remove a normal alarm from the app.

Modify the next alarm set to wake you up.

- If you've previously used the Health app to create a sleep routine, the Clock app's wake-up alarm will display the time that corresponds to the next wake-up time in that schedule. Even though you don't use Clock to program your wake-up alarm, you may still make adjustments to it after you've established a sleep plan and are using Clock.

   1. First, select Alarm, and then select Change.
   2. Modify the hours when you go to sleep and wake up.
      o You can adjust the time you wake up by dragging the Ringing Alarm button, the Bedtime button, or the semicircle that is located between the two icons. You can even adjust both times at the same time by dragging the semicircle.
   3. Navigate to the bottom of the page to see the Alarm Options, then make any of the following adjustments:

Tap the screen to deactivate or activate the alarm.

- Sounds and Haptics: Touch the screen to select a ringtone or vibration.

- To adjust the volume of the alarm, move the slider.

- If you need a few more minutes of sleep, you can use the snooze function by turning it on.

Turn off the next alarm set to wake you awake.

You have the option of turning off only the wake-up alarm that is immediately following the one you currently have set for your sleep schedule, or you can turn off all wake-up alarms for a sleep schedule.

1. First, select Alarm, and then select Change.

2. Go to the bottom of the page and select Alarm Options before turning off the alarm.

3. To finish, tap the Done button, and then select one of the following options:

- You Can Only Adjust the Next Alarm

- Feel Free to Alter This Timetable

Remove the alarm for morning.

By deleting or turning off your sleep schedules, you are able to get rid of the alarm that wakes you up.

Take action in one of the following ways:

• After selecting Change, navigate to the Health menu and select Edit Sleep Schedule. Finally, deactivate Sleep Schedule.

• Open the Health app, then either delete one of your predefined sleep schedules or deactivate all of them.

COPY PASTE

Copy, cut, or paste

• Copy: Pinch the opening shut using three of your fingers.
• To cut, close the gap between your three fingers by pinching it twice.
• To open a tube of paste, pinch it with three fingers.

You also have the option to touch and hold a selection before using the Cut, Copy, or Paste buttons.

It is essential that you quickly cut, copy, and paste your content into the appropriate locations.

SCAN DOCUMENTS DIRECTLY FROM YOUR IPHONE

Scan a document

1. Launch Notes and pick an existing note to edit or create a new note.

2. Click the button labeled Camera. To begin the process of scanning a document in Notes, tap the Camera button, and then tap the Scan Documents Scan document icon.

3. Position your document so that it is visible to the camera.

4. If you have your device set to Auto mode, the document you want to scan will be scanned automatically. If you need to take a scan manually, press the Shutter button on your keyboard. To scan, you can either press the Shutter button or one of the Volume buttons. After that, you have to drag the corners to adjust the scan so that it fits the page, and then you have to tap the Keep Scan button.

5. Either select the Save option or add more scans to the document.

Sign a paper

• First, launch Notes, and then tap on the attached document to a note.

• First, select the Markup icon from the menu that appears after selecting the Share button.

• First, select the Signature icon by tapping the Add button, and then either select a previously saved signature or create a new one. After that, you can change the dimensions of the space reserved for your signature, and position it anywhere you like on the page.

• Tap Done.

Follow steps 1 and 2 in order to manually sign your document. After that, select a tool to use, and manually sign the document using either your finger or an Apple Pencil with an iPad that is compatible with both.

CHAPTER 6:

Taking a look inside iOS16

iOS16 has recently been released by Apple, supported by the majority of iPhones (from iPhone 8 and later versions).

To update your phone:

1. Go on Settings

2. Select General

3. Tap on Software Update

But what are the biggest changes that are worth mentioning?

With its young predecessor, iOS16, a wide range of updates and features have been made available for iPhone users.

➢ Lock Screen fully redesigned. The lock screen now is highly customizable with a lot of options for widgets, effects, images, and animated wallpapers.

To customize your lock screen with the software's update:

1. Unlock your phone

2. Press and hold to bring up the option of customization

3. By pressing on the "+" button you will be able to add a new paper. You will have the ability to choose between featured, weather and astronomy related, emoji related, collections or color wallpaper.

➢ Focus mode: it is now possible to link this feature to different lock screens and set up different focus filters for specific applications.

➢ Notifications: they have been completely redesigned to take less of your display's space. Notifications now appear from the bottom and stay grouped. To open your notifications you can swipe up, or swipe down to hide your notifications.

➢ Dictation: with the update it is now possible to dictate texts in messages, documents. And the transition from dictation to touch has been made easier, with the keyboard staying open while you are dictating a message, making it easier for you to fix and edit the text, if needed.

➢ Live text: It is now possible to share videos, pause it while watching, highlight a text you see on the video to copy paste it or translate it.

➢ Maps app: the built in map application can now support multiple stops.

➢ Mail: it is now possible to undo mails, you can mark emails for follow up reminders, and it is possible to schedule emails to be sent at a later time.

➢ Visual look up: allows you to grab a subject of an image, isolate it from the background, and drag it on to another app. For example: a subject in a photo you want to drag into a text.

➢ Messages: it is now possible to edit a text after it has already been sent, undo or delete a message up to 15 minutes after the message was sent. Mark a text that you already opened as unread so you can remember to answer at a later time.

➢ Health up: feature of tracking medications, which comes in handy for everyone who needs to keep track of several medicines.

➢ Fitness up: it is now possible to use it even without owning an Apple watch. You can track your activities through this app.

Since the release of iOS 16, Apple has made several changes. The latest update to iOS is iOS 16.1.1 which aims to fix the bugs that users reported.

CHAPTER 7:

TAKING CARE OF YOUR PHONE AND FIXING COMMON ISSUES

iPhones, all Apple products if we had to completely honest, do not come at a cheap price. But with the price also comes the quality of the product, which is highly praised. Not only the quality, but the customer's experience is always taken into account. That's why it is always a good idea to take care of your phone in order for this to last long in time. Here are some few suggestions to take into consideration.

Battery

1. Keep your battery life between 40% and 80%.

2. Do not leave your phone plugged in if it's already charged. Leaving your phone plugged in can decrease the effectiveness of the battery because it gradually wears it out over time.

PROTECTING YOUR PHONE

Accidents may happen, it is not uncommon to drop your phone. The most annoying part is when a simple drop causes a crack on the screen or a big dent on the phone. That's why protecting your phone with a proper case is always a good idea, also never forget to protect your screen as well.

RANDOM RESTARTS WHILE CHARGING

A lot of factors could be the reason for your iPhone restarting while charging, but there are easy and quick fixes to this.

1. Force restart your phone

a. Press and release the volume up button

b. Press and release the volume down button

c. Press and hold the side button until the phone turns off

2. Update your iPhone to the latest iOS version

FROZEN SCREEN

If your screen freezes, the best solution for this problem is to force restart your phone. To do so:

1. Press and hold the volume up button

2. Press and hold the volume down button

3. Press the and hold the side button until the phone turns off and the Apple logo appears.

CHAPTER 8:
PRO'S TIPS AND TRICKS

APOLLO FOR REDDIT

If you love social medias, forums, and you are a big fan of Reddit, this little trick might interest you.

a. Download the app Apollo for Reddit

b. Head into the main settings of the application

c. Select General

d. Select Pixel Pals

If you turn this feature on you will get a tiny little pixel walking in the dynamic island while scrolling through Reddit.

ALWAYS ON DISPLAY

To turn this feature on or off

a. Select Settings

b. Select Brightness

c. Turn on or off the toggle for Always On

ACTION CAMERA

Open the camera app

a. Slide on the video

b. You will se a new action mode icon at the top right corner of the screen

If the action mode is turned on you will be able to change your resolution, HD or 2.8k, and change the frame rates.

AUTO CROPPING

Open a picture with an subject you would like to send without the background.

a. Tap and hold the subject of the picture

b. Select Share or Save if you want to save it as a new picture

LOCKDOWN MODE

This feature makes this new model of iPhone one of the safest phones around, its main goal is to protect your privacy and security. By turning this feature on your iPhone will block connections to your phone. This action is recommended only when you think your phone is being hacked. Tu turn it on:

a. Select Settings

b. Tapo on Privacy & Settings

c. At the bottom of the page tap on Lockdown Mode

d. Tap on Turn On Lockdown Mode

NOTIFYING EMERGENCY CONTACTS

This feature allows your phone to recognize a car crash situation you might find yourself in. In this case your iPhone will send you an alarm, which if failed to answered to will allow your phone to send emergency services to your exact location.

Made in the USA
Las Vegas, NV
03 April 2023